Empty Jacket

Vicky Bates

ISBN: 1523493658

ISBN 13: 9781523493654

Library of Congress Control Number: 2016904559

CreateSpace Independent Publishing Platform

North Charleston, South Carolina

The Butterfly counts not months but moments, and has time enough.

—Rabindranath Tagore

Prologue

1999

I feel the difference. First the rush of adrenaline pulsing and spiraling through my body, fear going down like burning coffee swallowed too hot. I steady myself against the emergency table that fits my son's body so perfectly.

Standing in a blinding room, I ask myself, why us? Why now? The doctors move quickly. Clipped, practiced talk passes back and forth with each instrument, as if an allegro is being played out over my son. I do not understand their coded language, only the urgency of it.

Three hours pass. Then the old walls of the community hospital vibrate as the helicopter lands next to the back door. There is no landing pad, only an extra wide driveway. The crew enters and rushes down the worn, green hallway in flight suits. I try to concentrate on a health poster taped to the wall and become a spectator watching someone else's tragedy unfold.

A back door is opened. The frenzied pace comes to an abrupt stop.

When did it become night? I close my eyes and inhale the darkness. The cold air swipes at me and does the only thing it can to help: wake me up to continue the fight. It will not let me be lured into hopelessness. I, alone, have the strongest desire to make my son live; I cannot give up. It is dark and silent now. Everything is unfolding in slow motion. My breathing slows; I try to focus. There is but one sound I hear in the night: my heartbeat weaving in and out of the droning of the helicopter. Suddenly everything is clear. This life and death nightmare is happening to my beloved child Rocky. I must become the deer in the forest that stands alert and frozen, as I instinctively know that my son's life depends on my honed skills, like those of the doe listening for the sound of the hunter's steps. I have to force myself to acknowledge what is transpiring, stay sharp, and not drift into shock and disbelief. It is as if I have stepped through the back door and into another dimension. No one could know by my appearance what lies beneath. My fear becomes the iceberg hidden under the surface of the sea.

Can we survive the fifty-five minute trip over the mountains to the city hospital, or are the doctors right in telling me the chances are extremely stacked against my son's survival?

I look up and view a shooting star crossing our path. I wish hard, as if it were yesterday and I still believed in such things.

Chapter One

1988

A woman I have only seen on video in my lawyer's office hands me the baby she delivered two hours ago.

Woman to woman, in a dim hospital room, we study each other as she passes her son over to me. I have waited forty-two years for this moment. No words can express this electrical current between such intimate strangers. The powerful mini-second when one person nods and hands over part of her being, part of her hopes, dreams, and lost love, and makes me a mother.

Years later I think about that moment and my son's spirit. What was happening in that brief instant? One woman carrying to term a baby she thought she would share with her lover, another woman waiting for motherhood and having no idea what that would entail down the road. The spirit of a boy touching two women.

We chose our adoption lawyer because a friend had recommended him. With thirty years in the business, he was a no-frills kind of guy. He looked like Alfred Hitchcock in a wrinkled suit and worked in a small Naugahyde office, similar to one you would find in an early detective film. We were nervous and had to explain to him, and then to his video camera, why we wanted to adopt, why we would make good parents. These questions took us totally by surprise. We tried to wing it and present what we thought was our best side as a couple.

"We're educated," Steve began. "We can financially provide a good life for a child."

I really don't remember what else he said because I was worried about how my hair would look on video after a hard day at work and the long drive. Suspecting that Steve's story was too analytical, I started by saying that I was a writer and an art major, all the time thinking to myself what a stupid thing to say. I might as well have said, "Hi, I'm Vicky and a Pisces. I like soft summer breezes and picnics at the beach!" God help me, I needed to think quickly and fix this while the camera rolled on.

"I can spend quality time with a child," I said.

I made up what I thought were good parenting skills, based on what I had heard or had seen on television shows. I wondered how many people who have birthed their own babies had to reason, analyze, and bare their souls like this to a stranger, a parental judge, a jury of one.

One week after our visit, the lawyer called. A woman who was nine months pregnant had come to him wanting to give her baby up for adoption.

"Meet me at my office within twenty-four hours to see her video, or I'll pass you over for the next couple," the lawyer said.

My husband, who was traveling, told me to go and check it out. Easy for him to say; he didn't have to face this caricature of a lawyer and his homemade video.

The next day I was sitting on one of the lawyer's straight-backed chairs. Nervously placing my feet flat on the worn carpet, I sat up tall, hands in my lap, and tried to act sophisticated and knowledgeable.

My lawyer, standing at the TV, turned slightly and asked, "Are you ready for me to start?"

"Sure, that would be great," I said.

He started the video. I certainly had talked the talk to Steve with great bravado, but here, in the office, it was a different story. My heart was pulsating with such force that I was sure it was revealing my inner apprehensiveness. I had to look composed and self-assured, or maybe he wouldn't select us.

From my peripheral vision, I caught the lawyer glancing at me. He was probably trying to gauge my reaction to the videoed mother. What an eerie feeling to sit and watch a woman who is possibly carrying a baby for you talking to you from a flat, inanimate screen. How could I make a quality decision surrounded by all this brown plastic furniture? How could I decide on my own? This was way too fast; didn't people wait months, years, to receive a baby? What about our much-needed vacation? Could she wait another few weeks? How did that work?

I stared at the woman as she talked about her life. She seemed sad but, thankfully, educated. She said she was Italian and raised a good Catholic—but not quite that good—as she patted her stomach and smiled. She interrupted herself often by crying, especially when she mentioned her boyfriend, who turned out to be married and an on-and-off drug user.

"What if the baby isn't healthy or has some major drug problems?" I timidly asked the lawyer; I was frightened by the woman's reference to drugs in the video.

"You do not have to take the baby if something is wrong," he said. That was the last time I ever brought that issue up with anyone. Didn't the doctors do tests? Later I would not dare speak of it for fear that would make it true. I could hear in her voice the hope that her lover would come back for her and their child, and now I could hear her deep pain. I'm sure that was why she waited until the last minute to walk into this adoption lawyer's office.

She said she had two years of college and wanted to go back to finish her education. I believed her desire to start over, but somehow I knew things wouldn't be different or better for her. Looking out from the screen at whoever happened to be out there, this very pregnant woman, with thick, brown hair down the middle of her back, smiled. I liked her; she could have been a friend. I left the office nervous and excited.

That night my husband called from New York to discuss what we should do. He said, "Maybe we should wait for the next baby to come up for adoption. This is way too fast. When I get home, we could see him again. Everything about that man and his office seemed odd to me. Maybe he's not on the up-and-up. Why did we meet at night?"

Getting frustrated, I said, "Remember you had a business meeting, and I had to meet with a client about some design work. He offered to meet us late; it was to accommodate us."

"I thought it took a year or two to get a baby," he said. "Remember what happened with that couple in Chicago? The court awarded that child back to her natural parents after the adopted parents raised her for two years. I think the real father came forward or something. We only have our neighbor's sister's word that he's good. These are uncharted waters for us."

I know he didn't want anything to go wrong for me. He didn't want me to get hurt or be disappointed.

Getting into this whole motherhood thing, I said, "I feel nervous about this, too, Steve, but I think we should go for it. Who knows when another baby will be available?"

If I had truly been honest with Steve, I would have acknowledged a few of my own apprehensions about being good enough to handle a baby, but I never let it surface. I was afraid to stress him out any more, so I glossed over the whole adoption. He could have very easily said, "If you have questions about this adoption issue, maybe we should reconsider."

When I jumped into something, I jumped in and asked questions later, even if I had doubts. I often operated on gut instinct. Steve was more methodical and thought matters through, which was probably a good trait when facing life-changing decisions.

The only truth I held dear was that if this was the right child, then that little spirit being was coming our way come hell or high water, and I would be there with my diaper bag and whatever else people claimed was important.

How bad could it be? It's just an infant, not a mysteriously wrapped package from Iraq addressed to "Any American Named Steve." Steve needed to lighten up that business attitude; this was a lucky break. Why worry about every little detail? There was always plenty of time to figure things out later. First we needed to get our hands on a baby.

Our differences were why we made such a fascinating couple. Steve was trained at a very young age to count his change and watch his back. His New York parents reminded him that there were always people lurking around to take advantage of him.

When he was young, his mom would say, "Go to the store and make sure you get a fresh loaf of bread. Don't let that Johnny guy push old stuff on you because you're a kid."

His family wanted him to know that everyone from the meat man to the police could be trying to pull a fast one, and they wanted him to always be one step ahead in case those people tried to muscle their way to authority. Now, years later, even going through the Tijuana border in Mexico, Steve would say, "Vic, I want to get through easily and not get pulled over for a car search. Let's not have any of your funny cracks when the inspector comes around to the car. You're the only one who thinks your jokes are funny."

I knew that wasn't true. I was very entertaining.

I vividly remember a Mexican kid shoving Chiclets gum through the window of our car, followed by a parade of brightly painted Blessed Mothers and Buddha's being thrust at us down the line.

We were next to pull up. Leaning over Steve, I smiled at the border man as I discreetly grabbed Steve's inner thigh and said, "Great day today. Can't wait to come back to your lovely country."

Finally the border control waved us on. Steve turned and looked at me and said, "You're too much!"

"But you love it, don't you?" I said.

The following Tuesday as Steve sat in his doctor's office and waited for a check up, he was staring at a glass coffee table covered with an assortment of magazines. On top lay an old *Sports Illustrated* that caught his eye. Flipping through articles, he found it hard to stay focused. The decision to adopt was looming over him, along with the responsibility of taking care of his wife. It was time to decide.

As he chatted with the doctor, Steve mentioned that he and I were considering adoption.

"No kidding?" the doctor said. "My two boys are adopted."

"It's a big decision, especially at our age," Steve said.

"I don't know what to tell you," said the doctor. "Our adoption was fifteen years ago with a lawyer who seemed a little strange, too, but he did a good job. His name was Mr. Fraser."

Steve practically fell off the exam table. "That's the name of our lawyer. I can't believe it. A fat guy with an ugly office in LA?"

"Yeah, that's the guy. He was different all right, but he had a good reputation with the state adoption agency. You can trust him. My boys are great, and we had no problems whatsoever with the adoption procedure."

It was fate.

When Steve came out of the doctor's office, he was relieved. After that, he had few reservations about the lawyer or the pending adoption. His mind skipped right over the dirty diapers and night feedings and focused pleasantly on teaching his child how to play his favorite sport—baseball.

We told the lawyer to go ahead. Two weeks later on a Wednesday afternoon, we got the call from our lawyer while we were working.

"I've been trying to get a hold of you two for over an hour!" he said. "Your baby has been born. Get up here. You have a baby boy."

Steve had been on a long-distance conference call about his wine-brokerage business, and on a different floor in our Orange-county office, I was on the phone, convincing a lady that she really wouldn't love a bright-yellow flowered sofa for more than a week. I had started my own consulting firm for interior design a year earlier. I mostly worked for large companies setting up boutiques in department stores for skate and snowboard companies. That job required traveling, so it was a welcome break to work on private homes in the area.

As I was hanging up, Steve came dashing into my office—his tall athletic body swinging around the corner of the doorframe, his tie flying behind him, and his green eyes wide open. He said, "We have a baby boy! He was born an hour or two ago! We need to get up there!"

It took me a moment to shift from a yellow sofa to a baby boy.

"What? Oh my God, we have a baby? Are you sure? Was he supposed to come now? It's a boy?"

"Yes, I'm sure; the lawyer has been trying to call us for an hour."

I hadn't even bought diapers or bottles yet. I guess the whole process was too surreal for me. I jumped out of my chair and ran for the front door.

As I flew by the receptionist, I yelled to her, "Mary, could you get a few baby things and put them in my house for later tonight? We have a new baby!"

"Wow…sure, like what?"

"Small diapers, powder. You know, the regular stuff."

I was thinking to myself, what was that regular stuff? I had asked about baby essentials a while ago. I think it was at the Fairbank's neighborhood cocktail party, but, in all honesty, I had been more focused on why Elaine was leaving her husband than on boring diaper-rash creams. Asking one experienced mom a baby question opened the conversation up to all sorts of dirty, sordid information. I think I truly believed that becoming a mother would never happen. Why else had I not bought any baby products? I guess the truth was that if the baby deal fell through, I didn't want people to feel sorry for me. I had a happy-go-lucky, sarcastic image to uphold.

"Oh, and something for him to drink," I said. "Someone said soy milk was good, and while you're at it, get something for all of us to drink. We have a baby!"

She was a mother, so I assumed that she knew what to get better than I did.

Forgetting my purse in my office, I ran out the door with Steve and hyperventilated all the way to the Santa Ana Freeway on-ramp. Now Steve was taking charge, and I was a wreck.

Two hours later we were at the city hospital and were riding in a small elevator, going upward toward a new life, starting in the maternity ward. A woman approached us as we got off the elevator.

"Are you the couple adopting the baby?" she asked in a loud booming voice.

This was like getting a call in the third grade to the principal's office over the loud speaker: "Attention! Attention! Would Victoria Ellen please go to Sister Teresa's office immediately?" This adoption process was uncharted water for us. Some things you just couldn't prepare for. Fear and excitement were in a dead heat.

"Yes," we said tentatively, wondering how she knew.

"Follow me."

"Ah, we'd better wait for our lawyer," we said. "He should be here any minute."

We were scared to enter the hospital room by ourselves. What if we did or said something wrong and messed up our adoption? What would we say to the mother, this stranger with our baby? I couldn't make small talk as if we were all waiting in line at a crowded restaurant. Would she ask us questions we weren't prepared to answer? It was one thing to see her on video and another to see her in person. Did she still want to give him to us? Would anyone else be in the room with her? We were self-assured business people, well traveled, in our forties, and we were scared to death to walk into a hospital room.

"You know," the nurse said, "you can go into the room without your lawyer."

"Yeah, ah, we know, but I think we'll...Oh, there he is. Mr. Fraser, we're over here."

He had been downstairs getting coffee and escorted us right into the room, fifteen feet from where we were standing.

There on her bed sat the birth mother, her dark brown hair down past her shoulders, like a large Buddha statue, holding a baby and chatting. A female friend of hers and that woman's son were standing on the other side of her bed. The boy, who seemed to be about eleven, took our picture. Could he do that without asking? I didn't want to say anything. The mother smiled and handed me her baby with such ease and grace that it was as if she were passing me an appetizer at a party. I looked at her with awe. As everyone watched, I took our baby in my arms. The boy took a picture of us. Tears started to stream down my face. I was a mother. I was holding our baby, our own baby boy. We were a family now.

The nurses gave us a little dimly lit room with two rockers in it so that we could bond with our son, who was five hours old. I held him for a few minutes and then gave him to Steve.

"Here you take him," I said.

He was so little and soft, with big brown eyes. He would open his eyes for a second, look at us, and then close them fast, pretending to sleep. He was too shocked at the looming faces five inches above him, with big Halloween grins and coochy coos. Yes, Son, we are your parents.

I had never even babysat for anyone. I guess it was a little late to be thinking about that. Could you break a baby? How could everyone trust us with his care so quickly? If the truth were known, we really didn't get this bonding thing. Was it supposed to be an instant revelation? We looked down at this tiny being whom we were holding so awkwardly. We were now responsible parents. So why then did we feel like we were in the *Mars Attacks!* movie, looking at an alien being? When was the nurse coming back in to take him and let the little guy rest? We needed a drink.

We named him Rockford, a strong name. My husband was figuring that he could be called Rocky, a good ballplayer name. I was thinking to myself, *I'll call him 'Rock.' He'll be a confident and sexy guy.* This had been decided over many dinners and drinks with friends and with conversations with deliverymen who had happened by our house.

After thirty minutes, we asked if we could go home with him. The nurse said, "Oh, no. He needs to stay overnight to be tested and signed out. Come back tomorrow." It was such a long drive from the LA valley to Orange County, and I was so emotionally wiped out that I remember telling Steve that I couldn't make that drive back and forth, even if they were offering us Baby Jesus.

We got a hotel room nearby and were back, ready to go, at the hospital the next morning, at five. We were in fact the only ones ready to go and had to wait until nine for doctors and social workers to make sure that the mother didn't want to change her mind. Why did they have to ask her again? What if she changed her mind?

We went down to get some flowers. How can you possibly begin to write a card? What do you write? Best of luck? Thanks for the baby? We wrote from our hearts, something simple: "We will cherish and love your baby as our own. Thank you from the bottom of our hearts for entrusting us with this precious gift, your son."

When I went in to say good-bye, she handed me a small three-by-five-inch ruled card. On it was printed, in pencil, a list of all her family health issues she could recall, such as asthma, allergies, diabetes, and heart problems. She knew nothing of the father's background except that he was Nicaraguan; she briefly showed me a wallet-sized picture of him. I felt strange leaving her sitting in that bed alone. She was so much more relaxed than we were. She smiled and wished me well and was ready to get on with life, while I was nervous, exhausted, and ill prepared.

When we were ready to go home, the nurses put Rocky and me in the back seat while Steve drove. I can still see Steve driving us down the freeway, talking to the rearview mirror, and saying, "This is easier than ordering a sofa."

If we had only known...

Chapter Two

Why did we wait until we were in our forties to adopt? We found out in our late twenties that we couldn't have children biologically. Suddenly I could not rely on staying home and just being a housewife and mother, which is what I'd planned on doing after college and burning my bra. I'd planned on setting a new standard: an educated, stay-at-home mom, ready for potlucks and running charities. I went to college in the late sixties. I was good at school, esoteric discussions, marching for causes, and circular Jell-O molds bonded with cream cheese. I was afraid of the possibilities of failure out in the real world. Oh, I talked a good story, but I had been raised to believe the worst. Like the old days with the Hare Krishna brochures at the airports, low self-esteem was handed out at every corner in our house.

I now believe there was a plan out there. It involved first small steps and then hurdles. Over the years I had not only one career but many: copywriter, stylist for photographers, interior designer, and clothing-store owner. As I became stronger and stronger, I discovered something interesting: me. Good positions were coming my way. In the beginning when I got a promotion, I would think, *Wait until they catch on and find out about the real me.* Because of my upbringing, it took many years of experience to realize that my abilities and talents could lead to success.

Steve experienced a different childhood in Queens. Over time I'd pulled out bits and pieces regarding his youth. It was so far removed from my life in the Midwest. My childhood was *Charlotte's Web*; Steve's childhood in New York was *West Side Story*.

I would go off on tangents about my childhood, but Steve's stories involved few words spoken at a snail's pace. Sometimes when I would ramble on and on, Steve would look me in the eye as if he were staring down a rabid dog, stick his arm out Hitler-style, and say, "Thank you very much. Next contestant, please."

This would make me laugh in spite of myself.

"Very funny, Steve," I'd say, "and what did you have to say that was so earth-shattering?"

Who was this mysterious New Yorker whom I found sexy? Steve was not interested in revisiting his childhood. I thought it just wasn't important to him, but as the years passed, I realized that there were things he wanted to forget.

It amazed me how differently we were raised, except for the binding link—sporadic affection from drinking fathers and troubled mothers. It was our different personalities that had attracted us to each other, but it was the underlying dysfunctional childhoods that bonded us.

◆ ◆ ◆

When we first got married, we moved from Chicago to Ohio. After a few years, Steve's company asked if we would move to California. Were they kidding? Despite living in a new, "solid" high rise, we had to open the oven door for extra heat. If a blizzard howled through, we would crank it up to broil. We couldn't wait for the warm weather and ocean breezes.

In California, we loved to hang out at the beach, read books, and take walks searching out tide pools, shells, and driftwood. Steve never questioned the weird stuff I would consider interesting and was always on hand to transport odd objects home for table decor or art projects.

Toward the end of the day, covered in that salty, summer glow that felt so good, we would go for dinners on a pier in San Clemente. Over a great meal of steamed clams and thick, juicy cheeseburgers, we would listen to the pounding waves come in, talk about trips and funny neighbors, and make plans. A few times we laughed about how we had met in a Chicago bar.

"Remember, Steve," I said. "It was an English pub on Rush Street. And it was the Queen's birthday, so drinks were half-price."

"Yeah, I was in there celebrating my buddy's graduation from Notre Dame Law School. God, that was the early seventies. We had been there most of the afternoon," Steve said.

Kathy, my college roommate, and I had just moved to the city. We were fresh out of school with new jobs and living in an old brownstone apartment sans furniture except for two beds, an end table, one chair, a mixed set of discarded family dishes, and two copies of *Catcher in the Rye*. At that time, I was making a measly salary as a photo stylist. That particular Saturday afternoon we decided to forgo buying the kitchen table we'd saved for and continue to eat standing up. We took off for Old Town, a hip area, and bought new outfits. I bought some short velvet, brown hot pants to wear with my brown, suede knee boots. I thought I looked hot; today they would call me a hooker. It's a frightening memory of the seventies.

"Remember, Vic," Steve said. "I approached you at the bar and asked, 'Do you live in the city? What do you do here?' And you just rambled on and on: 'I just received my fine arts degree. I was a painter, but there aren't a lot of paying jobs for painters. And I didn't want to teach art, so I'm working as a stylist for a commercial photographer on Ohio Street.' And then to shut you up I said, 'Wow, that's cool; I'm a Peruvian painter.'"

I thought to myself at the time that I couldn't believe my luck. Was this fate? I was falling in love. I overlooked the fact that you had a New York accent, were built like a football player with reddish-brown hair, and were drunk from an afternoon of celebrating with your buddies. What an idiot I was, and they say Dominican College girls were smart.

I liked a guy who pulled one over on me. I was used to being the witty one in a relationship, and this man was clever.

That night I said a strange thing to my roommate: "I think I'm going to marry that guy Steve. He's pretty funny."

Six months later we were married.

Over the years we grew more and more connected. He was always supportive of my dreams. What I loved about Steve was the fact that I was somewhat of a controlling person, and he was never threatened by my goals or ideas, only proud of me. I, on the other hand, loved that I couldn't pull a fast one on him. He was strong but very kind to everyone; he would always go out of his way to help someone, so much more than me, back then.

Steve was resolute about going into business for himself after moving to California, and we decided to give away the comfortable benefits of working for a company. This made me step up and get involved in a new job for a group of designer-clothing stores. I had to start as a salesperson. I knew nothing about clothes but was hired because I had sold expensive artwork. At the clothing store, I moved up and traveled around the country giving fashion seminars. I found my first true passion while Steve was getting his business established. My job helped us get through the tough times while Steve was starting out. He had a wonderful reputation for honesty and creativity in the industrial-ingredient world, but he was very humble about his knowledge.

Steve grew up in an old New York brownstone, similar to the one on the Archie Bunker *All in the Family* series on the television. All three levels had family members with spot-free linoleum floors and plastic-covered furniture. Even the lampshades were covered in plastic. Could it be that they had moved from a hurricane area and felt they still needed the extra protection against the rising tide? On the bright side, maybe they didn't need to dust; they could just drag the hose up a flight of stairs and spray down the living room once a week.

The top floor held his aunt and uncle's family. Steve's family occupied the main floor. Grandmother anchored the basement apartment. She owned and ruled the building that housed her two daughters' families and spent the days cooking and the nights drinking homemade wine, smoking nonstop, and playing cards. Mother Teresa she was not.

They all yelled at each other. I realized later that I was witnessing their conversational voices. Happy, sad, or angry, Queens always sounded the same to me in that house. Steve's dad was hard of hearing from the war. Men still didn't have the proper ear protection during World War II, and many times during heavy firing, they would stick their fingers in their ears to lessen the deafening sound. Between his loss of hearing and drinking problem, things got pretty intense at times. Every meal or conversation had to be shouted out. The family begged him to get a hearing aid, but he refused.

"Can hear just fine. What's a matter with you people? Besides, why should I get a hearing aid? Then I would have to listen to your mother," he said with a smile.

"But, Dad, then we could have a good talk."

"I just went for a walk," he replied. "Take your mother."

Of course he didn't need a hearing aid when everyone was yelling. When they didn't yell, he would think they were talking about him.

"What are you whispering about over there?" he'd ask.

Sitting there, I scanned the beautiful picture frames around the room; the photos looked familiar. I got up and took a closer look while everyone was conversing. As I zeroed in, I realized they were filled with the original forties movie-star photos from the store. Steve told me later that his mother would rather stare at Elizabeth Taylor and Tyrone Power than her own family.

The fights were always the same, only the linoleum floor's color changed from floor to floor.

During the fifties, Steve and his friends played stickball on their narrow street and would dodge between parked cars. At twelve years old, they bought cigarettes for two cents apiece from the corner candy store and put them behind their ears to save for a quick smoke after the game. Besides stickball, there was the delightful game of "knuckles," which gave everyone a chance to slam the side of the deck of cards across the knuckles of the person who lost a bet.

In grade school, one of Steve's jobs was to help Mr. Zuchelli, the florist. After school, he would run through the cemetery and collect all the week-old baskets, which had been purchased the previous weekend and left on the grave sites. This insured Mr. Zuchelli a steady supply of containers for the following weekend rush and gave Steve extra pocket money.

Central Park, with its rolling green fields and trees, was nowhere near Queens. Instead they had St. John's Cemetery, the only greenbelt, where the famous godfather of New York, Lucky Luciano, had been buried. Lucky's family shipped his body back from Italy, where he had been deported for underworld activities. This gave the neighborhood a local tourist attraction for days when company didn't want to venture into the city to see the Empire State Building. Visiting friends and relatives could easily take a leisurely stroll down the avenue past the beautiful flower shops with ready-to-go baskets for the deceased.

Queens was a movie set that remained the same scene after scene, take after take, generation after generation. In reality, there was nothing distinct about Steve's particular street. The cars stood across the same cracks in the pavement on Seventy-Ninth Street as they did on Seventy-Eighth. The mothers wore the same flowered housecoats with snaps running down the center, and all the blue-collar fathers worked close by. Everything looked, sounded, and smelled the same from street to street. The Polish and Jewish bakeries in each neighborhood filled the air with freshly baked breads. Many kids grew up, had children, and lived across the street or in the same house, never leaving the neighborhood, continuing the cycle.

One thing was for sure: no child could ever get beyond the high-frequency sound of the Queens mothers' voices screeching out of the windows. The dogs even cowered and ran for cover. All the children looked up, as if in a freeze frame, holding their positions and baseballs in midair when they heard a mother's yell. What a relief when it was someone else's mother, someone else's turn to run an errand or take care of a household chore. No mother worried about sending her children on errands down the street. The children didn't have one mother in the neighborhood; they had many. Everyone knew each other's kids and didn't hesitate to yell at any of them.

"Sammy, why did you send your baby brother in here? Didn't your mother say to play nice with him?"

"Mrs. B, he was ruining da game."

"Ruining your game? Well, Mr. Big Shot, you don't have to worry about that anymore...*home now*, and take your brother."

Steve's mom would yell for him to run to the corner store for some butter she needed for supper, and he would grab a kid as a stickball stand-in. These stand-ins would stand by one of the cars used as a base while he would run the errand in record time.

Another voice zoomed in from an adjacent building. "The trash is not going to move itself, Mr. Smarty, unless you want your father to move it after he's worked all day."

"Ma, this is a good game…just a sec."

"Don't give me that mouth, mister."

Squinting at his buddies with a bounce in his step, Steve's buddy Patsy Pompao would practice his ambling walk toward the stoop of his house and would try to appear casual, as if his mother's yelling wasn't embarrassing him in front of his friends.

In the summer of 1955 when Steve was fourteen, his life changed. His mother sent him to a working farm in upstate New York to get him away from the "street hoods," as she called them, and enable Steve to earn extra school credits. The farm family had healthy, long meals. They were full of discussion, in sharp contrast to Steve's experience of being handed a cup of coffee and seeded roll at the age of ten and pushed out the door.

After the morning meal, they all went out to their assigned chores. One day they would lift heavy hay bales warm from the sun. Another day he would help with the chickens. There were two thousand Rhode Island Red chickens, and they needed to be fed and their eggs collected three times a day. There were seventy cows that, after they were milked, would wander up the hills of the Catskills until evening when, on their own, they would return to stand at the barn doors to be milked the next morning. This was not easy, but it was a great lesson on how families could work together.

As the summer passed, everything fell into a simple routine. There was calmness in the country, with pastures of sweet-smelling grasses. Steve gained weight and confidence in the serene atmosphere.

When he returned to the neighborhood, the kids asked, "Steve, where ya been?"

"Oh, I had a job up north working."

Away from home, he had found a sense of self. Life became more than one city block and a handful of friends.

After that summer experience, he decided to go away to school as soon as possible to escape the turmoil at home.

At eighteen, Steve was his own man, in charge of his life. The future was wide open, and after graduating from college, he entered the workforce and traveled for companies with an adventurous spirit.

As years went by, business professionals called on him for advice. He was streetwise, with a quick New York sense of humor, and ready to read any situation; New York did that to people.

♦ ♦ ♦

My own family was an equal match. In our house, my mom and I were always trying to smooth things over and distract my father from money issues. Money was a full-time job. He was either counting it or worrying about it. Driven to be one step ahead, I was adept at drawing attention away from a potential fight by making jokes and clowning around. Because my dad owned a landscaping business in the Midwest, we were always riding in and out of a seasonal wave.

"It's spring. All our money is going out for new stock; nothing is coming in," my father would say.

"It's too bad you and your brother's birthdays are in the wrong season. Summer or fall would have been better," said my mother.

Was she serious? Was it our fault we had two Catholic parents whose rhythm confined itself to the tavern dance floors? That was the only place my dad took my mom for an evening out. In late spring, my dad's humor returned with the songbirds from the south. The season for play or rest never came.

"I'll rest when they put me in the box," he said.

When the business was back in full swing, he would hand us a large crisp, twenty or fifty dollar bill, which was a lot in those days, for no reason.

"Go buy yourself a little something; you deserve it," he would say.

This went hand and hand with the story "The Ant and the Grasshopper," which I had to retell continually.

"Do you remember the story about the ant and grasshopper?" my dad would ask.

There would be a long pause, as we would stare at each other across the blue, Formica kitchen table. It was show down at the OK Corral, and I knew I didn't have a chance of escaping.

"Yeah, I remember," I would reply. "There was this ant. He worked hard and saved his food for winter. Every day he put food away, never taking time to play. The grasshopper played all summer and thought the ant was stupid to work so hard and not enjoy himself. Winter came. It was cold. The grasshopper got very hungry. He went to the ant's house in the blowing, cold snow and knocked on the door. 'Please help me. I have no food, and I am freezing. Let me in, my dear friend.' The ant looked out of his warm house as the snow blew around the grasshopper and said, 'You laughed at me all summer while you played around, and now you want me to help you?' The grasshopper said, 'I am sorry; you were right. Next summer I will listen. Let me in, or I'll die out here.' The ant was kind and let him in."

At this point, my father would nod his head slowly and smile.

"Which are you?" my dad would ask.

"I'm a grasshopper that likes to play and doesn't save for a rainy day," I would say, knowing the answer he expected.

If the season were right, this would make him laugh and fill me up. When my father directed his smile toward me, it was like the drop of water given to a thirsty man. It was never enough, but it filled me with the childish hope that tomorrow would be different and that he would become more like the dads I saw on television and less like the ant.

As young kids, we always worked hard. We had the responsibility of cutting our acre of grass and weeding and raking the flower beds. One day my dad surprised us with a new riding lawn mower. Some kids received bikes. We got a riding mower. The funny thing is that my dad really thought that he was giving us a very special gift. When we didn't jump up and down with joy, he said, "Do you kids know how much this costs? Do you think Jim Nickerson bought his kids one of these mowers?"

We knew he would answer his own question given a second: "No, the Nickerson kids have to cut their grass the old-fashioned way and are damn happy to do it."

"But their lawn is really, really small. It takes Bobby about two seconds to cut his grass, and ours takes all day," we said.

My brother and I fought over who could use the mower first. That was the last time we ever argued about being first. After a few runs up and down the hill, the mighty green cutting machine lost its charm. It was too slow to take any foolhardy risks on, and we knew it was excessively stable, which left out wheelies. Nonetheless, we tried. Behind the row of purple and pink lilac bushes, behind towering walnut trees, or in the tall weeds, we did our tricks. Sometimes we cut the grass standing on the seat like performers in the Barnum and Bailey circus.

These tricks had one audience member, Sparky, the burly brown workhorse. Sparky would watch us go back and forth until we unloaded a fresh bag of newly cut grass into his enclosure. He loved grass almost as much as the marshmallows we cooked for him. Sparky knew what the word "hot" meant, as he had been burned once by a fresh-from-the-fire marshmallow stick. That big, fat, juicy nose would move up and down until he felt it safe to grab his treat off the stick and swallow it like a giant vitamin. Sometimes at night, Sparky would get out of his enclosure and eat our neighbor's corn or stare at her through her picture window. Mrs. Mirabella would turn from her knitting and see an immense nose pressed to her window and giant teeth hanging down like window shades. She would scream, and then she would get up and call us to come over once again and collect our horse. I think Sparky had a thing for her.

Since we were in the landscape business, our grounds had to be perfect. We not only had to weed the garden but also to shape the borders into clean lines. When we were trimming bushes, they had to line up as if they were soldiers standing at attention. My dad wanted us to be that ant family, but he might as well have tried to make donkeys into flying squirrels. It was not going to happen.

Another reason why I think my dad liked the yard to look good was the high-roller men's poker games he had in our basement on Friday nights, which he called the Wheaton Social Club. Dad built a box under his poker table where he could skim a chip from each pot to go toward refreshments and prizes, which everyone loved. At midnight, my mother would come down the stairs looking beautiful and carrying a multitude of items in her arms. Depending on the week, it could be a pot of barbecued beef or a roasted turkey or a ham with all the sides. She was like the hostess from *The Price Is Right*, pointing out the goodies and chatting with the guests during the break.

Once a year during the Christmas holidays, Dad had a drawing for the club members for a television set or, the most popular of giveaways, a trip for two to Miami. Everyone loved the Fridays in our basement and stayed until dawn. If my brother and I woke up early, we could spy on them. Sometimes I would go and stand

by my dad's side and anxiously wait for some sort of acknowl-
edgment, a smile or a touch. Other players would look up and
say hi. But only on rare occasions would my dad glance up, and
when he did, it was all business, asking me to retrieve something
or other. He wasn't a hugger or kisser. It's a wonder why I became
so touchy-feely with people; it certainly wasn't learned at home.
After getting the usual response, my brother and I would make
a leftover barbecue or ham sandwich and watch the Saturday
cartoons or Roy Rogers. My mother was not as perky, since she
had just cooked and served a big meal for a bunch of men at
midnight.

How my dad worked so hard during the day and then or-
ganized this poker night was not hard to understand. Midnight
snacks, raffle prizes (especially stamped poker chips), and people
coming over every Friday night gave him a sense of belonging and
vitality. He forgot about work for one night.

My mom was a simple person. She was a very spiritual woman
who always had a special affection for the Blessed Mother. She
and my father married early and had their fill of family tragedies
(as I would, too; it was one of the few traits we would have in
common).

When we were little and my dad was drinking, my mom kept
her sanity intact by lying down every day and saying the rosary.
Mary became her helpmate, and she called on her often during
the day when we were kids.

"Mother of God, you kids are going to kill me."

This phrase was interchangeable with "Mary of God, wait till
your father gets home."

I didn't appreciate God during those young years. I think it
was forced on me through years of Catholic school and being
told that there was a possibility of God turning against me for

lying to my mother or kicking my little brother. Time passed, and as I approached my thirties, I found peacefulness during mass. I felt the grace and calmness of all the people praying together. Part of the transformation was growing older, learning to meditate, and incorporating other spiritual beliefs into my life. Instead of always saying prayers, I just started having more conversations with God. I talked to him when I was happy or worried—or even when something made me angry. We became close; I'm sure he found my ramblings and jokes amusing and looked forward to them after a day of whiners. At least I was an entertaining whiner.

My dad always took the family to Sunday mass. Heaven forbid anyone lingered at church and blocked my father's car after services. He would have just been given a blessing, and now we had to move fast. Get to the car. Be the first ones out of the parking lot. If we were hemmed in, we would hear "God damn it, what are those people doing in there?"

We were always in a rush with my dad, never knowing why, anticipating the next shoe to drop. It was always hurry up and wait, even when we went out for Sunday dinner.

"What's taking that meal so long? Who ordered the fish? We are probably waiting because of your order. How long does it take to bring out a salad? My steak doesn't take that much time. Stop eating those crackers, or you won't eat your dinner. Where is that girl? No. You can't have another Coke. Drink water; it's good for you. Do you know how much those Cokes cost? Have one when you get home."

We were dizzy from all the rhetorical questions.

Eating at home was no better. During the week, he had to have lunch on the table at noon sharp. He was like the Peter Pan crocodile that swallowed the clock, always ticking as if he were a bomb.

Dad was trained when little to save every penny. There was no extra money. His large family lived through the Depression era. At his house, the blue-plate special always had to be a full hot meal, served precisely at noon. The entrée came with a vegetable, salad, and an argument on the side. Dessert and a kind word cost extra.

◆ ◆ ◆

My mother was beautiful. When I was young, people told me she looked like Ava Gardner. Smiling down, they would say, "Why, honey, you look just like your daddy."

Friends thought maybe she had been in the movies or modeled. Before she was married, she used to always wear a fresh flower tucked in her hair; she was especially fond of gardenias.

I was tall and skinny, a walking Q-tip with a cotton candy head, thanks to my mother who tried the newly invented Toni home permanent on me. One thing you do not want to hear your mother utter when unrolling those smelly, drippy rods from your aching little head is "Boy this perm was much faster than I thought!"

When I look at early pictures of my father, he was very handsome in a William Holden sort of way, but the years of hard work and drink changed that. He had a great intelligence and wit, which he often put to paper. He was quite funny as long as you weren't the target of his jokes. When paying business bills, my father enjoyed including a snappy letter to the wholesalers, whom he knew by name and family history:

> "Dear Hines Brothers Nursery,
>
> It is lucky you have a sister in the family who decided to become a nun. Someone needs to pray for your souls with the prices you charge! Enclosed find a check for the maple trees."

"Dear Crooked Tree Farm,
       You call this shipment Grade A straight? What
did you stake them with, cork screws?"

Honing my own sense of humor from his example helped tremen-
dously when I became a mother. I used humor as a protective
shield when things seemed out of control or when emergencies
came up.

It wasn't always intense with my dad. In the winter, our basement became a vacation getaway. The scent of Coppertone
drifted up to our kitchen along with the sound of Mitzi Gainer
singing "I'm going to wash that man right out of my hair," from
South Pacific. We were drawn like bees down those red linoleum steps to view my dad in an Adirondack chair of his making, basking under a sun lamp, wearing nothing but khakis and
Coppertone, and smoking a cigar. He looked so content, almost
peaceful, but he was a mystery to us. On good days, he would
share the adventures of his youth, which we pulled out of him
word by word.

Some nights I would catch a glimpse of him sitting hunched
over on the side of his bed; his head hung in his hands and rep-
licated the lonely side of *The Thinker*. What demons took him so
far away at those times? He had severe asthma and owned and
worked in a nursery with abundant health triggers from the now-
banned pesticides. He smoked cigars and drank to excess. He
was always short of breath and constantly using an asthma inhaler that never seemed to work, which made him even more up-
tight. I was glad, at the time that I would never have to experience
asthma; it scared me.

Every morning my dad would stand at the sink and fix himself
a glass of Alka-Seltzer. Back and forth between two glasses, he
would pour the potion until it had mixed with water. Like a mad

scientist, he would drink it quickly, relieving whatever ailed him. We knew he wasn't going to talk to us until he returned at lunch. The tension at meals was probably due to a hangover, but we always thought we had done something wrong. We sat there looking at our sandwiches with those hot searing rocks nestled under our little rib cages.

When my mom needed a rest from us, she took us to the farm, which was about twenty miles away.

"Guess where you two are going?" she'd say. "On vacation to Grandma's farm for a few days."

"Why?"

"Because I need a vacation."

"Why?"

"You can take your dog, Duchess, and Pretty Bird Boy with you."

Only thirty minutes by car but another world away, the farm became my refuge. Growing up, it held a space within me. I could go there in times of sadness and could dial up the sweetness and kindness of another place and make of it more than it was, like the boyfriend I didn't care that much about until he left.

Grandma was short but substantial, built for strength like a John Deer riding mower. Her hair was white and braided into a bun at the nape of her neck, and she was way ahead of the supermodels with the layered-clothing look. Grandma had no patience for wasting time changing clothes in the heat of the day. So early in morning about five, she would head out into the cool barnyard wearing the following:

- Men's gray work pants, tucked into
- Tall, black rubber boots, over which settled a

- Flowered, print dress and a faded cotton
- Babushka, which tied under her chin and covered her beautiful round head.

She told us who Santa was and taught us how to make holly-hock dolls from the garden. She alternated between motivational fairy tales about the "old country" and tealeaf readings, which she could only do when my grandfather was nowhere to be seen. It was evident to me that my grandma was very intelligent because she taught her German shepherd to understand Polish. I couldn't comprehend how that dog was smarter than me.

Grandparents are always nicer to their children's children. Patience comes with knowing that someone will eventually pick up the little darlings and whisk them away, out of sight.

Sometimes Grandma, who was from the old country, couldn't pronounce words or mixed them up.

She would say, "Chilwren, come and eat sum ice-a cream and cakie. You good kids, come."

Once she made a pineapple upside-down cake.

When it was time for dessert, she asked, "Who wants yunky-dunky cake?"

We dared not look at each other; my father would repeat it dramatically.

"Hey, kids, how about some yunky-dunky cake?"

That's when we couldn't stand it anymore, and we laughed so hard that the milk started to squirt out of our noses. Some families played ball together; we sharpened our table manners at Grandma's.

Grandmas and mothers handed down their techniques for raising children by example. I approached motherhood first by ignoring it, and then as I got older, I thought that I would decide when, where, and how I would raise my kids, end of story.

Chapter Three

When we first moved to California, we found out that we couldn't have a baby. We really weren't that interested in starting a family, but when I went for a checkup, the doctor asked what I was using for birth control and I said I hadn't for a while. She was curious as to why I hadn't got pregnant since I was off the pill. We were playing with fire.

I remember going out to lunch after a morning of testing to see if we still had a choice about getting pregnant. We were told we couldn't make a baby. We were in shock and said little during lunch, thinking our own thoughts. Why was it that if we weren't ready to start a family—didn't even know if we wanted a family—all of a sudden a stranger saying we couldn't was a startling announcement? We had taken for granted that we were in charge of our destiny when it came to children. Our right to decide was not in our hands anymore. Not thinking there was a way to have a child without a multitude of tests and disappointments, we said that it wasn't the worst thing that could happen and that we would concentrate on our careers. We loved each other and were great friends, and maybe now we had time to take a trip to Europe and move on.

Nothing was said after that morning. That night I went to bed thinking about what the doctor had said and wondered what was going through Steve's mind, but I didn't ask. Why was our right to choose taken away? It was so final. As time passed, we never talked about it and decided to immerse ourselves in our professional lives. Once in a while, I would take pause when I saw a cute toddler and would wonder what could have been, but it never was a nagging feeling that could change my thinking.

We were in the process of planning a contemporary clothing store in a major shopping center. I was designing and buying for the store, so the word "child" ceased to enter my mind.

I had worked hard and was finally realizing my dream.

I had to wonder if I was subconsciously following in my dad's footsteps, driving myself to excel at business. I wanted to be the top sales person, an outstanding storeowner and best designer. I worked long hours to prove my worth to customers, friends, and myself; it was the same way I had tried to impress my father and get praise years before. Steve and I both worked hard. We traveled extensively for business and fun and truly enjoyed each other's company. We had been married for eighteen years. Steve got my sarcasm and gave it right back. At times conversing was like a Ping-Pong match.

When you do not have children, you have the selfish ability to act as if you're still dating. Holding hands during quiet dinners followed by the latest movies, no preplanning. We were growing up, becoming wiser and more self-assured. Our friends had children, but those small beings seemed to be an interruption in our otherwise-smooth life. Then something happened. We got older. And unexpectedly our business lives took a dive. The glow was off the buying trips to Europe for me. I was exhausted from the pace. I was always calculating what were going to be the upcoming trends, duty taxes, and shipping into the country and then coming home to run the store with employee, customer, and leasing problems. Steve's import business dipped because of market changes.

Was there a bigger picture for us, or was it all about day-to-day business and weekend plans? While friends were watching their children take their first steps, we were reading the Sunday

New York Times and figuring out where to have brunch. I believe that it was then that a kind of grace, unbeknownst to us, started to seep through a crack down into the crevices of our bodies under all that fat, muscle, and grizzle, way in the back corner of our hearts. A baby was patiently waiting for us to grow up and see what was important. He would have to wait only a few years.

Wherever we went—whether together or alone, on business trips or vacations—we came across people who were in their forties and fifties and had just adopted a child. At the worst financial time in our lives, we started to think we should consider adopting a baby. We had always thought there were many babies who needed love and a home. Based on my Catholic/Buddhist philosophy, which I had honed over the years through reading and meditation, I believed that before a child is born, that little spirit being selects his or her parents based on the lessons the parents and children have to learn together in this lifetime. My husband's philosophy was "whatever," as he would roll his eyes and glance at our friends. At other times, Steve would smile at me and then go back to reading his paper or book as if he had a secret. I could not engage him in any of this dialogue. He was a tough, up-front New Yorker, and I was a Midwest flower child of the sixties. He was not into spirit talk and babies floating into your life. Meditation for him was that moment before a golf swing.

♦ ♦ ♦

As our eighteenth anniversary approached, we started to ask around, rather casually at first, to see if anyone knew about the adoption process. Adopting was a way for us both to be fifty-fifty in the process. It was like going to buy a car together, or so I thought. We never had a particular profile in mind when we began our search for a child. Steve and I were open to whatever would come to us.

Ordering up a blue-eyed, blond baby to look like us was something we never even thought of discussing. It seemed silly. The baby we would be given was the baby we were supposed to have, no matter what kind of package he or she came in.

I never understood why people said you should adopt children who look just like you! To me, a child should float down into your life like a dream with his or her magic, not yours. That is what I believed.

And that's what happened. A brown-skinned baby, with long legs and a skinny body, a baby who didn't know the word "float," came blasting into our life like a Scud missile.

Chapter Four

Everyone was eager to see what the Bateses had brought home. As we drove up our street multiple walnut doors started to open, neighbors slowly started coming out. No one in our community had any idea that we even wanted children. They were shocked as they entered our home and spied a naked baby in the middle of our four by six foot dining room table.

There we were, the successful, on-the-go couple, standing at the hand etched glass table that used to shine brilliantly. All of us were in disbelief. The table was transformed from a dust-free work of art to command central. There were stacks of diapers like chips at Vegas. Baby blankets, creams, T-shirts so small they reminded me of slices of white bread, bottles surrounding a small changing pad. Covered in baby powder, this whole tableau looked like a drug bust gone bad. I had no time for cute teddy-bear changing tables that first week. I needed room to work my magic on my skinny, large-nosed, brown baby, who lay in the middle of the table like the main entrée at Thanksgiving. People were watching me in disbelief as I rolled up my sleeves and attacked the problem.

I stared at him in wonder and hoped that he would grow into his body parts—a worry I couldn't verbalize to people in case they thought me ungrateful or, worse yet, unmotherly. Now that he was home with us, I started to get more insecure and nervous. Did we do the right thing? I think we did. With all my earlier bravado, I certainly couldn't mention this to Steve. So why was it so hard to believe that this Rocky baby was staying with us to be cared for *forever*?

Everyone trusted us with his new life—the hospital staff, the social workers, and the birth mother. Were they fools? We were overwhelmed already, and we had just got home with him. What would happen when everyone left?

I was trying to change Rocky's diaper when my dear friends Sue and Laurel stopped by. Sue, an interior designer, had two young boys, and Laurel, a hair-salon owner, had four girls and a boy. They were my inspiration. Both women were beautiful, calm, and strong. They kept up with their careers while being great mothers—something that seemed important to me at the time, as I had been a career woman for so long and was now starting the mommy business in my forties. I decided to take time off from work until I got this baby thing under control. It would probably take a week or two at most.

The three of us were squeezed in my bathroom and were trying to change Rocky's diaper.

"Oh, look at his tiny little penis," Sue said; she loved every baby she ever met.

"It's not tiny. Why would you say that?" I replied, tears filling my eyes. She had had big Wisconsin Gerber babies. Was she thinking something was inferior about my Rocky's maleness? Could adoptive mothers have postpartum depression, too?

When everyone left, Steve and I tried our hand at the disposable diapers. It was not as easy as it had looked. If you tried to adjust the sticky tabs, you could only reapply them so many times. Who would have known? We had put a company together. We didn't need directions about diapers. Not wanting to waste another diaper after two or three tries, Steve ran and got masking tape. I held Rocky up in the air under his peewee arms. Steve quickly ran tape around and around Rock's tiny body, as if he were headed for the last FedEx pickup.

"Look at him; he's wondering how he got such stupid parents," Steve said.

"Yeah, he is looking at us funny."

"Get the camera!" we said in unison.

It seemed that every day we had drop-in visitors to welcome our baby and get a look at him. In my whole life, I had never been so tired and stressed out from lack of sleep and fear of screwing something up. Why couldn't I be more like those pretty, smiling TV moms? Instead I just wanted to meet friends at the door in my smelly, flannel pajamas; take the presents; say, "Thanks, I'll be sure he gets this"; slam the door; and go back to bed. If they really wanted to take such a good look, why didn't they take Rocky home for a week and really study him so that I could get a handle on this mommy stuff?

When Rocky was a few weeks old, we took him for a general checkup with our new pediatrician. Rocky was to have a circumcision. Did I want to hold him during this procedure? Not really, but I figured if he could handle it, I should at least give my support. How bad could it be? We were led into a miniature exam room, and I was asked to sit at Rocky's head and comfort him. Steve was standing in the corner, looking up at the ceiling, and talking about baseball.

"Boy, did you see those Dodgers last night?"

I was rubbing and kissing Rocky's head. The doctor brought out the instruments. They looked like something I had seen on the Home Shopping Network. I was wondering if we would get a free set of steak knives to take home.

"He won't remember this," said the young doctor.

I knew the circumcision would be tough, but somehow our doctor being gay made me feel that Rocky was in the right hands. I was taking my new role as mother very seriously. Rocky's future depended on it, and I wanted "it" to be perfect. I felt I could witness anything after that procedure. Little did I know I would have to.

Rocky, we discovered, was not good at sleeping. Many mornings I would sit at the kitchen table and try to wake up after getting only a few hours of sleep. The night before with my eyes at half-mast, I had swayed back and forth in front of the French doors, tried to keep myself awake, and showed Rocky the stars or the moon. Many times I would catch myself just as I was about to doze off and fall into the fireplace. To stay awake, I started to sing Frank Sinatra's "Fly Me to the Moon." Maybe I needed to learn some baby songs.

When Rocky's crying finally eased, I felt as if I had suddenly entered an empty church at night. A deep sigh escaped my lips. He always needed such tremendous soothing. I thought he just didn't like to sleep, but friends started telling me he probably had colic. Could this be the only thing bothering him? On some deep level, I believed that he must have realized that the heartbeat he was hearing was not the heartbeat he had heard for nine months. Where had it gone? As his ear rested against my chest, did he feel confused and abandoned, or did he sense that the rhythm he was now hearing was the beat of unrelenting love, a love that would last forever?

"He must have his days and nights mixed up."

Did you ever notice that for every problem, there are a hundred "professional" answers by nonprofessionals? How did everyone get so smart? I finally understood what Leo J. Burke meant when he said, "People who say they sleep like a baby usually don't have one."

At our second visit to the doctor when Rocky was about two weeks old, I mentioned that he kept waking up every hour at night and crying uncontrollably for long stretches of time. When he did sleep, he slept through everything. The doctor walked over to my son, who was sleeping in my arms, and theatrically banged two loud objects above him and—nothing. He continued to sleep.

"He needs to be tested as soon as possible."

"I don't know if we can handle a deaf child," said my husband.

"We've waited so long to adopt," I said.

We both had tears in our eyes and a sense of dread.

This was right before Thanksgiving weekend, and we couldn't have him tested at the major eye and ear hospital in Los Angeles until after the holiday. The waiting seemed endless. We cried. We told no one but my mother, who always seemed to have a direct link to God; maybe he would listen to her. We prayed.

My husband and I had delayed this commitment to raise a family. Now we had a deaf child. I tearfully told him that I had once heard of a deaf football player, that there were no limits to our son's life. Surprisingly this did not cheer Steve up. We sat through Thanksgiving dinner and tried to act happy for our guests, who cooed over Rocky. With nerves like time bombs, ready to go off when least expected, we made idle conversation about football and cranberry recipes.

The day of the test arrived. We awoke early to beat the LA rush-hour traffic; we could not afford to be late. After entering the hospital, we were led to a quiet chamber, where our son was wired to a computer. Everyone left the room. The door was closed, and I was left with my son to sit and wait. I remember rocking him back and forth, wires attached to his head, and looking out an oversized glass window at the technicians and my husband's sad face.

The testing could not begin until he was asleep (not one of his best talents). I wore out God pleading and the Hail Mary prayer that morning. We waited.

He finally slept.

They tested the first ear. It was fine. They tested the second ear. It was perfect. What joy and relief we felt. The doctor told us that Rocky probably only had fluid in his ears and that it would soon disappear. In the unadorned hallway, I looked at the other parents, all vacant-eyed with fearful thoughts, with their babies. They sat there in the corridor and prayed their own prayers. I hoped that they would be as lucky as we were that morning.

That night we went home to celebrate. As we turned on the blender to make margaritas, we heard a loud "wah, wah." That was the first and last time we ever enjoyed crying.

◆ ◆ ◆

Our pediatrician told us to make sure that everyone who touched our baby washed his or her hands first. He was always warning us about something or other. He was a new doctor, who must have just finished reading *Everything that Could Possibly Go Wrong with a Baby, Tell the Bateses: They Know Nothing, and It Will Paralyze Them with Fear*. This book was found at popular stores in the entertainment section: "Ways to Have Fun with Patients at Parties."

The reason people were supposed to wash up was that visitors always touch a baby's hands, which are the first thing babies put in their mouths. Having only a small medical background on an index card from Rocky's birth mother's side and not even knowing the father's history meant that if Rocky were to get sick, the doctors would have to put him through extensive testing. Always being the perfect hostess, I felt uncomfortable asking our guests to wash up for fear of offending them. Plus seasoned mothers weren't so protective. So I directed no one to the sink and immediately washed Rocky's hands when everyone left. I had a lot to learn about motherhood.

Rocky was not a healthy baby. Looking back now and putting the pieces together, I can see that his crying was not because we were inept parents. I came to believe that there could be a possibility of drug withdrawal. Rocky never slept through the night for two years. His difficulty was compounded by allergies and severe asthma. He threw up violently from certain foods, had two or three seizures before age one, and had diarrhea often. Mothers who use drugs can strip their babies of their immune systems, which often makes the air they breathe and certain foods they eat poison to their tiny bodies. Doctors never brought up anything to warrant my fears about Rocky having any drugs in his little body. They said it was just allergies, asthma, or maybe flu. They were doctors. They would have known, wouldn't they? If he had drugs in his body, he suffered so needlessly. He should have been put on withdrawal medicines when he was born had that been the case.

♦ ♦ ♦

At about four months, I was walking Rocky back and forth when, out of my kitchen window, I spied two nannies chatting and pushing baby carriages by my door. I clutched Rocky and sprinted for the door, pried it open, and ran down our California-mission-style entrance.

"Do you know anyone who can help me with housework and watch my baby a few hours a day?" I asked.

"*Como?*"

"All righty, then...*amigo para me baby y limpiar casa?*"

"Oh, *si` mi amiga es muy buena and che looking pour a hob.*"

"Does she speak English?"

"Yes, berry good, like me."

"Can you have her come *mi casa manana*?"

"OK."

The next day there was a knock on my door, and there stood a short, smiling-faced woman in her forties. She had the look of a saint and came like the Lady of Fatima to help me. I wanted to fall on my knees and grab her dress; one touch of her hem could deliver me from this sleepless hell. Rocky cried every hour and one-half or more. My nerves were shot. And my blissful marriage was starting to resemble a scene from *Who's Afraid of Virginia Wolf?*

Rosa gave our whole family a sense of peace with her smile and kindness. She had two older daughters and knew everything there was to know about comforting crying babies. During her time with us, she eased many of our first-child fears, and because she had slept all night, she would always jump in to help me if needed. Just having a small break in the day was like a piece of heaven. Even though I took a leave from my design business, I couldn't catch up with my rest.

Would it have been easier for us to be in our twenties and not in our forties? I am sure we would have had more energy in our twenties and thirties, but with Rocky's colic, asthma, allergies, and general screaming problems, we needed patience more than energy, and as older parents, we probably had more patience.

At six months, Rocky had his first trip to the emergency room. One day we had taken him to the pediatrician for a bad cold. The doctor suspected asthma and gave us medicines. He told us to watch for worsening signs and to get up during the night to observe our child. First stage: chest expanding in and out. Second stage: stomach moving in and out. Third stage: shoulders pulling up and down as he tried to get some air. That night somewhere between the stomach and shoulders, I knew it was time to rush Rocky to the hospital. We pulled on some jeans and took off.

Steve, Rocky, and I charged into the Orange County Emergency Room only to find it packed as always, with standing room only. The receptionist, looking disinterested, slowly handed us a form though the window as if we were checking a coat. I pleaded for attention and realized I had to figure out the hospital ropes with this woman.

The Ropes

1. You have to be shot point-blank in front of her while holding up your Blue Cross insurance card, with your ID number visible.
2. You have to be having a third-stage asthma attack while holding up your Blue Cross insurance card, with your ID number visible.
3. If uninsured and unable to speak English, sit down and get comfortable. Someone will come for you sometime soon.

When they took a look at Rocky, he and I got into an examining room within a few minutes. The ER nurse said, "Follow me," and she showed us to our room. She dramatically pulled back the curtain for us to see what we had won. Our prize was a worn-out, white-sheeted bed accompanied by many plastic tubes hanging from bird-feeder-like metal poles, trays loaded with needles and vials, and oxygen masks and a stretcher hung on the wall as if they were pieces of art. Jars of big Popsicle sticks and gauze patches lined the metal sink counter in the corner. We could not see the worst element of the room: the distinct smells of fear, pain, and medicines. Each time you inhaled, your breath caught and reminded you that you weren't home.

The doctor entered, and Rocky was immediately given a shot and started on breathing treatments, which consisted of asthma medicines to open up his airways. When he didn't respond as they anticipated and was still pulling hard for air, he had to be admitted for a few days. It wouldn't have been so bad if a hotel bell captain could take you right to your room and you could order up room service and a pay-per-view movie. But first I had to proceed to another building and wait to fill out admittance forms while Steve waited in the ER with Rocky. Then I had to go back to the first building to the X-ray department, where Rocky and I waited against a wall of cement blocks in a darkly lit basement. I held him to my chest as I sat down on an orange plastic chair, on which someone had drawn a blue ball-pointed heart with "H loves P," and waited to be called for chest X-rays while people coughed and hacked all around us.

The multiple tests for babies were barbaric. For example, they held his arms down and locked his tiny baby body in a metal clamping device to take X-rays. He screamed in fear as they had me leave the room. There he was by himself, clad only in a diaper, in a cold, dark space, with all the hulking machines and the roar of that giant X-ray machine. I could hear him screaming for me outside the door as I sat and waited, my own chest tightening from fear.

Both of us just wanted to be comforted and go home, far away from this dark, dank underground corridor with the flickering overhead lights and sickly people.

Who had pointed the proverbial finger and decided to exclude us from that lucky club of families taking a calm stroll along the neighborhood lake, with the ducks and warm sun filtering through their bodies? We deserved to be part of that fraternity of tranquility and safety. I wanted to be the von Trapp family from *The Sound of Music* (only edgier and with better outfits) singing on the hilltops and skipping along, arms intertwined.

Why couldn't we just relax and enjoy the ride through my son's childhood as if we were a "typical" family? In some ways, this craziness was an extension of Steve's and my childhoods, where at any moment a disaster could be on the horizon. I realized later in life that we had really never known normal in our families, but one thing was true: it prepared us to think fast on our feet. Retrospect is illuminating.

◆ ◆ ◆

Finally the nurses brought Rocky out from X-ray, and we went back to the front desk to wait for a room to become available. By then I was so exhausted from the stress and lateness of the night that I just wanted to sleep. I wanted to send Steve home. It made no sense for two of us to pace, and there was only room for one parent to stay over. I made him leave.

"You have a big meeting tomorrow, Steve," I said. "We'll be fine now that we're at the hospital. I can handle this."

"I don't mind staying here. You can go home and get some rest. I don't need a lot of sleep," Steve said.

"No, you go. I'll call you if something else comes up."

Twenty minutes later we were given a standard green room. It was cleaned and mopped about three in the morning, which made the tiny patients cry. I got the chance to stay up all night and watch my son twisting and turning from the adrenaline pulsing through his body. I won the opportunity to see other children in pain and the grand prize: a chance to feel alone, sorry for myself, and once again angry at my husband for doing exactly what I asked him to do, go home and rest. I would stay with Rocky. I was afraid Steve would fall asleep, because as usual he was up so early. I was sleep deprived also, but I knew I was too nervous to sleep. I was the lioness watching her cub. Make no mistake about it.

A hospital never sleeps.

Once in the room, we started with IVs and blood tests. The nurse couldn't locate a vein in his arm into which to insert the IV (a difficult job with those cucumber baby arms). After many tries, she decided to put one in that beautiful, down-covered head. It wouldn't go in.

While he was screaming, she said to no one in particular, "If he wouldn't cry so much, I could get this needle in!"

I wanted to yell at her, but that was against my other hospital rules.

Other Hospital Rules

1. Be nice to the people helping your child, no matter how they treat you.
2. Never, ever leave your child alone and unattended.

There we were—he with his arms and legs tied and staked out to the crib bars so that he wouldn't pull out the IVs and his tiny face looking to me and I sitting in a cracked, plastic mustard-yellow chair pulled up to the crib and holding his baby fingers. Our blue and brown eyes locked, inches apart, unable to sleep. Morning would finally come and with that, the doctor's words: "I think you two can go home after one more asthma treatment. I'll give you a few prescriptions to take with you. Keep giving him treatments at home around the clock for another twenty-four hours. Check in with me Monday morning at my office for a follow-up."

"Thank you, doctor," I said flatly, with nothing left to give.

I have to admit that at times I preferred going to the hospital. Even though it was very stressful, long, and grueling, to put it mildly (and that was just checking in), it took pressure off me knowing other people were helping with the responsibility of keeping my son alive.

I watched the doctor leave as I stood there with my wrinkled clothes, messy hair, and drawn, tired face. And to think a few years prior I never left the house without lipstick. After about ten minutes, I traveled down to the nurse's station to find out what had happened to our discharge papers so that we could head home. Rocky was still not out of the woods with his asthma, and I wondered how Steve and I were going to stay awake that night to check in on him. My friends Suzie and Laurel had said I could call them if I needed help. But they had busy lives with kids and work, so how could I ask them to come over and do night watch with me? Laurel was the one who had told me how children would change and enhance my life when I was pondering adoption. I smiled to myself as I thought that maybe she would like the first night shift.

Absent-mindedly, I stood there. My hands wandered over Rocky's legs. They were like a well-worn map I knew so intimately. I ran my fingers along the markers of his childhood and paused at the scars, as if they were sweetly remembered places visited before. Those legs, which had stretched up to oh-so slowly inch the candy off the top kitchen shelf, were now quietly hanging over the hospital gurney.

Suddenly Father John materialized in the emergency room. The tiny room was like a dull green vortex sucking in numerous people—nurses, doctors, the hospice worker, and now our priest.

Wasn't it his dinnertime? Who had thought it necessary to call him? Rocky would be OK.

I wanted to be polite and say a few words, but nothing came to me. After Rocky received his blessings, all I could mutter was "Thank you, Father," as he looked up at me, solemnly nodded, and left the room. Rocky would be remembered in prayer and tomorrow's morning mass.

I whispered to the hospice lady that I couldn't talk to anyone else. I needed to concentrate on my son.

Chapter Five

Every time we rushed to the hospital, it was as heart stopping as that novice trip, and it always seemed to happen just when Steve left for an out-of-the-country business trip. I felt so alone, exhausted, and burdened with the responsibility, but I had no choice. I was all Rocky had. I remember so clearly the reckless driving through the night, down the Five Freeway, with a boy gasping for air who could not be soothed and possibly could die. It never got easier. I always wondered why police never stopped me as I sped along and zigzagged in and out of traffic.

Giving treatments every few hours, rocking him, watching for worsening signs at home, and mentally timing how long the drive to the hospital would take at certain hours of the day were just too much. When I knew we had to get to the hospital because a treatment had not improved his breathing, I would strap his teeny body in his baby seat and place him in the front next to me. I needed Rocky by my side to watch and rhythmically pat while maneuvering through traffic. Driving at top speeds with one hand on the wheel and the other gently and rhythmically patting his chest, I would keep whispering sweet words to calm him and me.

This certainly was not the motherhood I had expected, since my life as a businessperson had always been filled with effective problem solving. People had listened to me. Even people older than I. What was wrong with my child and the doctors? There had to be a solution to these health dilemmas. I was starting to hallucinate about those leisurely Sunday brunches as I walked back and forth every hour, every night, with a screaming child in my arms.

People would ask, "Are you sorry that you decided to have children after being married so many years, with a good career and free time?"

Never. Of course I would be lying if I said life was perfect. I wished it were easier. I wished that I had a healthy son without all the worries, but as I looked at Rocky, no amount of sickness could dissolve my devotion to him. I had to remind myself that on a spiritual plane we had selected each other to evolve ours souls.

I know my neighbors loved their kids but had been a little envious at times of Steve's and my freedom. They could not understand why two seemingly content people would suddenly, after so many years, seek out a child. The Bateses had a Porsche, didn't they? Wasn't their life perfect already? How were two older people going to handle a baby? What did a forty-something career woman know about babies?

Nothing.

As very hard and constant as motherhood was, with one touch from that little hand on my face, I was a goner. The beauty of a child's love slowly changed us all for the better. Every day there were lessons learned and always the kindness of the unexpected person when you needed it most.

One time I was at the pharmacy, leaning against the white, worn plastic counter and absently staring at all the Chap Sticks, sunscreens, and Trojan packages. This is a chain-store strategy for people waiting in line—last-minute purchases. A guy, picking up his wife's migraine medicine, might say, "I'm picking up a prescription for Mrs. Jones, and hey, I might as well throw in these Trojans," as he might be thinking to himself that maybe she'll feel better tonight.

Sex was the last thing on my mind. I couldn't even remember the last time I had felt sexy. One time I told my husband I had a headache, and his laughing reply was, "Don't worry; I don't need your head."

When I glared back at him, he said, "You have no sense of humor."

"I married you, didn't I?" I still hadn't lost my touch.

With all my sleepless nights, if Steve gave me that what-about-tonight look or—the tricky one—asked if I wanted a back rub, I would soon realize it was a ploy. I would either pretend I didn't hear him or say, "OK," and lay there half-attentive, trying to be sexy and thinking about how to get stains out of baby T-shirts. I couldn't help myself; it just wasn't so exciting when you were exhausted and waiting for your kid to scream. Another piece of the parent puzzle my friends forgot to tell me about is how your marriage shifts.

What happen to the on-the-go couple, who wore black designer clothes, traveled around the world, ate at touted restaurants, and made love on Sunday afternoons?

Another time I found myself standing in line at the same pharmacy while my mind was on asthma medicine. When do you give it, and how much do you give? Asthma medicines hype kids up; they have to be given right before sleep so that when they kick in, the child will be drowsy. Many nights I misjudged this, and Rocky and I would sit up all night in our pajamas on the living room floor and watch his favorite *Bambi* movie for the hundredth time.

"I had a sick child, too, honey," a complete stranger said, patting my hand. "He'll grow out of it, and before you know it, he will be off to college."

"How old does he have to be to go to college?"

She laughed and said, "Be patient. I'm sure he is a beautiful baby, and I can tell you are doing a wonderful job with all the health problems you have to deal with. Bless you."

That encounter meant so much to me. As she walked away, I thought I would cry.

From then on, I tried to verbalize kind thoughts about others when they seemed stressed or sad. Burdens and problems can be wrapped so tight inside us. We become like a balloon ready to burst with anxiousness.

I got my medicine, returned home, and hoped to get some shut-eye. When I got there, Steve and Rocky were laying together sound asleep. I envied them sleeping in our warm, comfy bed. They were so peaceful looking. I grabbed a pillow and headed for the sofa, and I fell asleep listening to the beautiful quiet.

◆ ◆ ◆

Once in a while, Steve would come home from a successful business deal all smiles after a few cocktails and eager to share his meeting. Of course I would say something like, "Oh, that's great, honey; you deserve it," but resentment was slowly building. With a gleeful lilt to his voice, he would ask, "How was your day with Rocky?"

Once, standing over his dinner plate, I pointed a brimming spoonful of whipped potatoes at him and said, "Do you *really* want to hear about my day? Do you, *Steve*?"

I was becoming Dirty Harry. Do you recall the movie where Clint Eastwood aims a gun at a bank robber and says, "I know what you're thinking, punk. Did I fire five or six bullets? Tell you the truth, I don't remember. Now you have to ask yourself do I feel lucky? Well do you, punk? Well, do ya?"

Steve was not feeling lucky. As he gazed into my eyes, his deserved good mood collapsed.

He stared up at me, took the serving spoon out of my hand, and placed it back in the bowl. He told me to sit down, and then he handed me a glass of wine. He wasn't a mind reader. After I freaked out, I felt instant remorse. My ego wanted to handle the daily problems like the perfect moms I thought were out there. What was I thinking? What was I trying to prove? It wasn't fair to Steve to let my frustrations out on him.

"I'm sorry. So you said you had a productive meeting today? Who was there?" I said slowly, as I sipped my chilled Chardonnay and forced myself to relax and focus like the Buddha (who I'm sure didn't have kids; otherwise, he wouldn't be sitting there smiling).

It wasn't as if Steve were hiding in the garage behind the dryer every night, drinking a cheap six-pack of beer, and reading *Playboy*. Why didn't his life change as much as mine? I took care of all the details with Rocky's health, and the more I assumed the position of foreman, the more I was counted on to be the foreman. Sometimes when I got back into bed and saw Steve sleeping, I would hit him on the head with a pillow. He hardly ever woke up from this. If he did turn and mumble, "What? What? Do you need something?" I would say, "No, no, go back to sleep; you're dreaming, honey." This form of amusement helped my nights pass.

The mere fact that Steve could fall asleep while I was still giving the martyr talk really annoyed me. Why did men get the gift of sleep?

Steve was more than willing to get up whenever Rocky cried or needed a half-hour asthma treatment at night. But I would say, "No, no, I'll do it. You have a big day tomorrow; I can take a nap in the afternoon." You start to do it so much that you become too efficient at your job, and then you are stuck.

All those years of Catholic school were not wasted on me. No sir, I could dish plenty of guilt and control. I was working toward being the first Catholic saint in the new subdivision of Irvine, California. Mommy and Me class in the morning, followed by sainthood in the afternoon. If I couldn't get sainthood, I could win a prize for being the oldest mommy in Mommy and Me. No one else had problems with circulation when crossing her legs on the floor during share time. It was painful seeing the women's young naïve faces, all shiny and bright, across from me. They might have been ready for an organic-apple-juice break, but this mommy needed a martini.

Stress could show up at our doorstep anytime, like an unwanted relative. There was no more leisure time; every minute was accounted for, day and night. I had to be alert. The On Duty sign was always lit. I was ready to be summoned, twenty-four-seven. Steve and I still had that deep connection, but we communicated more like mimes, with hand signals and eyes. All I can say is that we were lucky that we'd had eighteen years to grow together because after Rocky came into the picture, we needed a strong foundation to hold on to and, above all, the ability to laugh at ourselves and bounce back.

The only thrill we got was an occasional trip to restaurants, which included our son most of the time. One time when Rocky was about one, I remember studying a cute, young waitress at our local Mexican restaurant. There I sat like an old Hollywood has-been starlet—my eyes squinted, hunched over the table, and feeling very surly. This was a place where we could get big drinks with straws for fast relief, which I would pay for later.

"This will take the edge off," Steve would remark, as he would hand me a double margarita. As soon as we placed our order, he would say, "Check, please."

"No coffee? No desert for you this evening, sir?"

"No, just a check when you get a chance. And put twenty percent on for yourself."

Before the waitress took off, she zoomed in, put her face down near Rocky's, and said, "Your son is *so* adorable. My boyfriend and I want to have lots of babies when we get married. They are *so* cute."

Rocky tried to grab her earrings while staring at her big breasts, perhaps thinking that maybe they held a special candy prize (didn't all males live with that fantasy?). She had so much energy and no circles under her eyes; she must have been in high school, although she had to be old enough to serve alcohol. Why, God, have you surrounded me with all these young, dewy-faced, full-of-hope women since I became a mother?

I wondered how "Perky Breasts" would be after nursing a few kids. No one cared that Not So Perky Now always had spit up on her T-shirts and never had time for makeup or for shaving her under arms and legs on the same day. She would hurt her brain trying to figure out what had gone wrong with her marriage and why her husband didn't like Hamburger Helper anymore. She should have listened to her mom and become a stewardess.

"Vic, I asked if you were sure you didn't want some coffee."

"What? I'm sorry. No, I'm finished. I just need some sleep."

Too tired to show teeth, we smiled our big smiles up at her. Steve's technique was foolproof. As a top salesperson, he was always one step ahead of the client. If Rocky started trouble, Steve could be out immediately of his seat and have the car backed up and running, like a cop on his way to a robbery in progress. He could not stand for his child to disturb anyone; he was trying to be a thoughtful parent.

Lunches with the girls were easier. More children and moms were out and about. Before Rocky came into my life, this is what

I pictured my life as a mother would be. There I was, in my mind's eye, pushing my magazine-worthy, silky hair behind my ear as I bent down to tuck junior's blanket in under his chin so that all could get a better view. I would have no bags under my eyes, and as a "trendy" mom, I would have the latest stroller and black, designer diaper bag. I would not have throw-up spots on my navy Donna Karen blazer as if a pigeon had landed on my shoulder. People would become tiresome to me as they mobbed around and pushed into each other just to get a glimpse of my baby.

The reality, which Suzie and Laurel never told me about, is that first you have to prepare for an outing like planning a week-end vacation to a different climate zone. Upon arrival at the shopping center, you have to get all that stuff out of the car you just put it in, pop open the trunk, and get the stroller out. After this is all set up, you hold the stroller in place with your leg stretched out, foot hooked into the wheelbase, while opening the back door to retrieve your baby, who has finally fallen asleep after being up all night and now wakes up screaming.

You can't use the handy escalators you were used to before baby.

"Can someone tell me where the elevator is? Hello, miss, do you work here? Does anyone work here? Honey, Mommy's here. Stop crying, honey. Ma'am, can you tell me where the elevator is on this floor?"

You get to the allocated floor, push through the tight maze of clothing rounders, and knock off hangers and pants that hit your baby in the face, which causes him to start up crying again until you realize that he is crying because he has a dirty diaper, which needs to be changed on the floor you've just left. You are now late to meet your friends for lunch. You go back to the elevator, this time pushing the stroller with one hand while holding the clothes out of your child's face, and head for the ladies room. The restrooms now have baby-changing tables and sitting areas for nursing mothers. I think if I had to nurse, I would kill myself.

One woman actually said, "You know, I was reading that there is a way for adopted mothers to breastfeed. Wouldn't that be a great bonding experience for you and the little one?"

Was she nuts? I was with my son twenty-four-seven already. I didn't want to bond with him anymore than he wanted to have extra bonding time with me. We passed that stage the second night home. I didn't want the little guy to start screaming when he saw my tired breasts; it could push him over the edge. I had been growing my hair down to my breasts, but my breasts were winning the race.

Men never thought such thoughts or did lunch, and thank God, Steve never took any of those cross-country trips to Grandma's house, given his aversion to disturbing people. Planes really accentuate a baby's crying, and there is absolutely nowhere to hide, unless you are changing a diaper in the stainless-steel soup bowl they call a sink. On one flight, as I was swaying back and forth and trying to keep my balance between aisles, a well-dressed grandmother glanced up at me.

"Honey, everyone here was a baby once. Relax; they'll get over it."

"Well, they have three hours and twenty minutes to try," I said, helplessly.

Women are different. Women can eat a meal, drink a glass of wine, and discuss breast implants while their children are dancing on tables. Men have to fix the problem and find a solution immediately. If only men could relate to these situations as they did during a football game—totally focused, as if you were not in the room yelling, "The hot wings are on fire in the oven! Call nine-one-one!"

Sometimes there is no solution. It was certainly easier to eat at home, but eighteen years of dinner and drinks on a whim made it hard for us, the old yuppie parents, to never eat out. At least I think we were young enough to be yuppies. All those years of marriage definitely had made us more self-absorbed.

Then: "Do you want to run to the bookstore before the movie?" or "How about driving down the coast for an early sunset dinner?"

Now: You stand on your porch, wave good-bye to your neighbors, who are headed out to dinner, and return to the house, feeling a little sorry for yourself. Inside, you head down the hallway to check on your sleeping beauty before picking up a book or magazine. Maybe there is something good on television. A noise comes from your son's room. Someone is babbling. You walk in and are greeted by a teeny, uncorrupted smile. You pick him up. He slides his little starfish hand down the back of your shirt for security, and there it rests, warm and surprisingly powerfully attached to you, as if he is the gas-station man filling you up with love.

Chapter Six

This baby business was not a nine-to-five job. I realized that, like Suzie and Laurel, all mothers had a secret code that they used when talking with women about motherhood. It was like the *Stepford Wives* movie when they tried to entice you into the fold. When I asked what it was like to raise a baby, they never divulged the fine print. I only saw the baby ads and the cute Baby Gap models and thought this could be my life. How hard could it be? After all, some of these women had never even worked outside the house.

"Oh, a baby will change your life. Those wonderful little beings add a new dimension to everything, such a blessing," friends would say.

No one mentioned the dark side. They actually wanted you to see for yourself that life was not about dinners, freedom, and photo ops, but it was about throw up and diapers with poop oozing out like an over-roasted s'more. These friends were like the heroin dealer getting you hooked: there was no turning back from the powerful addiction to loving a baby, no matter how difficult it could be.

It seemed as if I was up every hour, heating formula and never dreaming that soy (something a nutritionist friend thought I should use because of allergies in the birth mother's family) would be a problem for Rock. It wasn't until many months later that we found out he was extremely allergic to soy products, which gave him terrible stomach cramps and diarrhea much of the time. When I would give him a bottle during the night, he would fall asleep in five minutes. But in a short while, he would awake, screaming. After walking him for twenty minutes or so, I would ease him down into the crib, sneak out, lie on my bed, and wait for the next "wah" to come. This usually happened in less than an hour.

Next I moved to plan two: the forbidden microwave oven. This was much quicker, although it was banned in the baby bibles. Besides, who would see me at three in the morning? I would microwave the bottle, shake it, test the milk on my arm, and hope for the best. Even though this was faster, it still wasn't fast enough for me, who, even under the best of circumstances, could never fall asleep easily. Third idea: I heated the milk and put it in a big pump thermos by my bed at about eight o'clock. When Rocky cried, I pumped a bottle of milk, as if I were a soda-counter specialist on a busy Saturday night, and ran across the hall to feed the hungry crowd of one.

"Maybe it's the milk, and he's allergic," said a neighbor.

"Maybe he's hungry, and you need to put baby cereal in his bottle," said another.

"But isn't he too young? The doctor said—"

"Oh, they don't know everything. Every child is different," she said.

One night after getting up about four times, I decided to try the baby-cereal route against the doctor's wishes. With only a tiny, hall night-light on, I poured Gerber's rice cereal into the baby bottle. I couldn't see well, but I feared any light would really propel him into a crying jag. All of a sudden, there was screaming and wild twisting in my arms. Terrified, I turned on the light and looked down. There on his face was a perfect, three-inch cone of cereal flakes covering his eyes and nose. I brushed it out of his eyes and off his nose and then turned him over and lightly shook him. He squinted at me through the cereal flakes stuck to his eyelids. At that moment, I could hear him thinking, *Who the hell screens these people anyway? What a bunch of frigging idiots I'm living with. If I could only use the phone.*

I cleaned him up and placed him in our Graco swing to settle him down. The Graco swing, an invention that should be up for the Nobel Peace Prize, is also called "Forget About Your Troubles." At six in the morning, five hours later, we woke up to see him still swinging back and forth, in and out of a slice of sunlight coming through the bedroom drapes. Could you damage a kid's brain by having it swish back and forth for so long? Time would tell.

◆ ◆ ◆

When Rocky was almost one, we started down a road of emergencies, ambulances, and races to hospital. Slowly and unfortunately, we would become experts.

It was cold. I pulled the covers over my shoulders and crawled deeper into bed. Steve, who was always up early, would listen for Rocky and feed him the moment he heard that blood-curdling scream coming from Rocky's room. How I loved my sleep. As Steve would say, "You are not a nice person when you don't get your rest."

What an understatement that turned out to be. I turned over on my side and tucked my hands under my squishy pillow, and there, staring at my eye level, was my child, Mr. Rocky Bates, in his red-fleece pajamas.

"Hey, what ya doin', buddy? You got out by yourself?"

As I reached out to pull him up on me and cuddle him, his body went stiff in my arms. His head fell back, his eyes rolled upward, and his mouth was frozen shut. I thought he was dead. My heart was pounding wildly in my chest.

I yelled for Steve, "Call nine-one-one! Call nine-one-one! Something's wrong. Rocky stopped breathing. Oh my God, Steve help me. Hurry."

I sat up with Rocky lying across my arms and tried to pry open his mouth. I didn't know CPR, but I had to try something, anything, to get oxygen in him. His mouth wouldn't budge. I thought he was dying. I screamed for Steve again.

"*Steve*, did you call them? Are they coming?"

"I'm on the phone now; they're on their way."

What was happening to Rocky? The paramedics kept us on the phone while I kept trying to open his mouth before he died on us.

Steve came racing into the bedroom with the phone to his ear and said, "They say to place him on the cold tile floor in the kitchen and take off his pajamas and diapers."

He grabbed Rocky and rushed him into the kitchen, where we stripped him down as fast as we could.

Finally I heard sirens in the distance, approaching our area.

"Oh my God, Steve, can they get through the security gate?"

"They have the pass number, but I'll run out and direct them to the house. You'll be OK here a minute?"

"Yeah. Go and hurry."

Rocky started to move, open his eyes, and come back around as the paramedics came through the door and surrounded him on our floor. We couldn't believe our eyes. He was back to looking naked and cute—our baby boy—and was awakening to three very tall scary men in heavy, black fire wear, carrying all sorts of boxes and tanks. The paramedics gave him a big smile and asked us if he had been sick. No, he hadn't, but we would head to the doctor's office as soon as possible.

After taking him to the doctor, who found nothing wrong with him, we monitored Rocky the rest of the day, but he acted as if nothing had happened. Unlike his parents, he seemed to bounce back from these incidents ready to engage with us.

The doctors were perplexed. The pediatrician told me that seizures also occur in children with epilepsy or autism but not to worry; he didn't think that Rocky had that problem. Great. How reassuring. One day when Rocky was eighteen months old, the seizures disappeared. Unlike their sudden arrival, they left quietly without ceremony or notice. There was only the indelible image etched in our minds of his still body and vacant eyes.

There were many good memories. One thing I think all mothers have in common is dressing their babies up for an outing. I remember one particular day Rocky when looked so cute that we headed for the supermarket. Pausing at the ground-beef section, I leaned over into a lady's cart and said, "What a beautiful baby," just so that she would say the same about my son. Do you know what she said? She said, "Where was he born?" I admit he was a little darker than most kids in our neighborhood, but what was with that about? Look at her. As they used to say in New York, she certainly was no looker. And I might add, it was obvious that the child she was pushing was hers, what with that big nose.

Right then I wanted to tell the truth. I wanted to say that her baby was ugly and that I had only said what I said so that she would compliment me on my precious, who was truly a work of art.

Oh, how I loved my son. Rocky had a load of health issues, but in some ways, I loved him more for his brave struggle. He was perfect in my eyes. He was growing into his chin and nose! He had beautiful brown, wavy hair, thick long lashes, and huge brown eyes that followed you everywhere. And oh, how he looked in his Baby Gap clothes. Please. I thought of sending them pictures to use in ads. I'm sure I was the first mother to come up with that brilliant idea.

Looking for dinner inspiration, I continued my stroll down the aisles. Von's supermarket was a block from my house and the place to go when I needed milk or adults in a hurry. I could get a few groceries, look at magazines, and chat with neighbors and strangers. Rocky didn't associate a good time with the grocery store. Whether it was the bright lights, the towering, red-aproned employees, or the drop in air temperature on my favorite frozen aisle, I will never know. What usually happened was that after I would place his car seat in the grocery cart, there would be a short period of quiet, which would be followed by five minutes of sniveling, whining, and twisting in his car seat and then followed by a high-pitch wailing. I'm sure the only thing keeping the store-front windows from shattering was the industrial tape holding up the pot roast and canned-corn specials on the glass. Usually, as eyes stared at us, I would retrieve a juice bottle and stick it in his mouth. It did the trick today.

As he sucked on his bottle, I headed for a cookware demonstration, where there was a sale on aluminum cookware. I had burned a few of my pots by melting baby-bottle nipples to the bottom of the pans, so I now had a set of nice rubber coasters but no bottle tops or saucepans. I approached an older clerk and looked at the sale items.

"I thought there was some evidence that cooking with aluminum caused Alzheimer's disease," I said, proud of the fact that I was an aware consumer.

The blank-faced sales clerk paused and said that he had never heard of that study but that if I had any problems, I could return the set.

"Well, if I have any problems I won't remember where I bought the set," I said, amusing myself with the unintended joke.

"Up to you. I just work here, lady."

This was no fun. The juice bottle was almost empty; the baby outing was officially over. It was easier just to buy another dozen bottle tops and return to the safety of our home.

Even with his fragile health, Rocky's gift for music and his sheer intelligence shone through. His birth mother might have given him brown eyes, but we gave him love, humor, and wit, which go a long way when you're driving people nuts. Yes, most times he took pleasure in embarrassing me in the grocery store by screaming as I raced up and down the aisles so as to get out fast. Then on the way home, he baby sang loud and clear with my opera tapes. He would only sing along with women, not men. Gazing out the side window and swinging his little feet back and forth, he was happy as a clam, as if nothing had happened.

Looking over at him, I passed our house and headed out the parkway. He was still smiling at me and swinging those legs. It was so wonderful to see him happy and content. If he could feel this good all the time, then he could really enjoy his life. It wasn't his fault.

What was he pondering as he scanned the scenery while we cruised down the country road? When we slowed at a light, I glanced over. Was he old enough to gloat over his power in the grocery store?

At that moment, he seemed too darn sweet to be sly. As if he heard my thoughts, he turned and smiled broadly with his big brown eyes and reached out to touch me. It was hard to keep up.

After a forty-five minute drive, we made a U-turn around some large eucalyptus trees, headed home, and passed two speeding fire trucks with sirens blasting. I turned to point them out to Rocky, but he was sound asleep.

◆ ◆ ◆

It was dinnertime the night I thought my father died.

Whenever I hear sirens, my chest tightens. This began when I was small, when the nuns and our mothers asked us to say a prayer every time we heard a fire truck or ambulance. It was late fall. The storm windows had been put up. The trees had lost most of their foliage, and with the time change, we now had our early supper in the dark. My mom was keeping the dinner warm for my dad when the phone rang. I followed her into the hallway, where she turned on the small metal lamp that sat on the telephone table. My mom picked up the phone, and with a look of disbelief, she yelled, "Oh my God, the ambulance is rushing your father to the hospital!"

She had me get down on my knees with her and say a Hail Mary. Our old, chubby neighbor, Mrs. Zondler, who lived across the street, put me to bed. My mom rushed out. I think I was having an anxiety attack, if a five-year-old was capable of that. While everyone assumed I was sleeping and not old enough to understand what had happened, I was in my bed unable to breathe too frightened to turn my face, which was buried in the pillow. The room was dark but for a sliver of light from the doorframe. I could hear quiet conversation each time the phone rang. Why didn't someone check on me? I was powerless to move any part of my body. Had my daddy died?

He had stopped after work to pick up a pizza and have a few drinks with the boys. On his way home, his car had run under a semi, which left him crushed and trapped. He had gone through the windshield and been caught under the truck; it took over an hour to free him. The firemen and paramedics finally got him to the hospital, where they gave him the last rites and had little hope of survival. In those days, children could not visit patients in the hospital, no matter what the relationship. After a week, I started to doubt that he was all right and would be returning to us.

My mom took matters into her own hands and decided to sneak me in the back door. The hospital halls scared me to death. Walking intertwined in her full skirt, I held on to the flowered fabric as if I were part of the pattern and peeked out at times or hid when a nurse went by. Were people looking at me, or was it my young, fragile imagination? What would they do to me, those women in the white starched dresses and hats, if they caught me visiting my daddy? Even with reassuring whispers from my mother, I felt completely vulnerable. My heart was pounding as we entered my dad's room; there wrapped in bandages, he sat and smiled down at me. He was alive. A week later he came home.

During the fifties, not many people talked about drinking problems or admitted they had a problem. Rehab centers were not as prolific as today. He convalesced at home for another month. He sustained internal injuries from the steering wheel and major head trauma from the windshield. He quit drinking after that accident for maybe a year. But he was an alcoholic, and even watching the beer commercials on television was difficult for him.

My father's family had no sympathy for him when he returned. One morning while I was playing in the yard, I saw my grandpa and uncle drive up. They waved to me, and I followed them in. From the small entryway, I could see dad sitting in his favorite chair in the living room. My portly grandpa plopped down on our beige tweed sofa. Grandpa observed my dad and said, "You look OK to me. When you coming back to work? We need you."

Not waiting for an answer, he turned to stare at the TV with his grown sons. I never witnessed any affection in our families, not even a handshake. After a long silence, my grandpa continued to talk to the television about how it was time to "get going and stop feeling sorry for yourself."

They expected him to pull himself up by the bootstraps and continue working. It was his duty. Alcoholism was just a bad habit, as Grandpa surely knew from experience. Everyone told us prayer would help. It wasn't until much later that God invented the Betty Ford Clinic.

For many years afterward, my father would not talk about the accident; he'd only mention the glass that kept working its way out of his forehead, month after month.

"Do you know why glass keeps coming out of my head after all this time?"

I stood there with my mouth slightly ajar and waited for him to answer his own question.

"Because it's pure and causes no infection. After a while, it slowly works its way out. But some pieces may never come out." He spoke efficiently, as if he had just given a science lecture to college students.

"Hmm," his audience of one answered. Another warm and loving father-daughter chat.

Chapter Seven

Someone is screaming. Is it a bird? No. Is it a plane? No. It's Rocky Bates. My eyes popped open. It was not a dream. The clock by my bed read 5:35 a.m. I'd been up with him for hours in the night, but like every morning, this sound came on schedule. It was as if I were standing on the runway as Delta's 10:10 flight to Kennedy made its final approach.

I pulled myself from bed, and just as I was heading for Rocky's bedroom, the telephone rang. Should I get the phone first? It wasn't as if it were the first time Rocky was crying. I ran across the cold, white, tile floor. This gleaming hard, white surface was not baby friendly. It was for the image, not for the baby or a child learning to walk. Who would have thought?

"Is everything OK over there? I heard Rocky screaming. Can I help with something?"

My son's cries were so loud that he woke up the neighbors.

"Did he wake you?" I said. "I'm sorry. These houses are too close together. Remember when we both had baby monitors on and we could hear each other's conversations through the walls of our houses? Thank God we weren't talking about each other! You pay all this money, and you're only feet from your neighbors."

"So you're OK with Rocky?" she said.

"Yeah, you know, I mentioned his crying to the nutritionist, and she thinks it might be low blood sugar in the morning and… and I'm rambling. I better go and get him…sorry."

"Well, good luck. See you later."

As if anyone wanted to hear my boring repetitive saga at 5:35 a.m.

I raced down to Rocky's room and picked him up, but he couldn't be calmed right off. What was wrong with him? Was he hungry? How could he be hungry? He had been up all night drinking formula. Was this normal and my friends had just failed to mention this quirk about babies at dawn, or was I doing something wrong? No one had an answer. I think I had exhausted all the friends I knew with children. Where were the answers? Where was Penelope Leach when you needed her?

During those endless screaming nights and tantrum days, I had an awakening of sorts to mothers who cracked after giving birth and shook their babies to quiet them down. I saw that in some sort of whirling, fanatical nightmare, they became different people from lack of sleep, tremendous stress, and even their own hormones. I believed I could never do such a dreadful thing even on my worst days. I was blessed with an education that hopefully helped me think things through, a good environment, and loved ones who supported me on hard days. Steve made sure I had friends and babysitting support when he traveled, and we had no lack of food in the house, rent-due problems, or financial worries. But there were days when I wanted to hand Rocky over, like any mother does, and thought I couldn't handle him for one more minute. I could understand the tipping point of stress; it could knock on anyone's door at anytime.

When an acquaintance would tell me about the terrible mother on TV who didn't deserve to keep her baby, I would be silent. No one supported harmful behaviors, and it made me ill to hear of an innocent child being hurt. But no one knows the whole story.

Maybe the mother had had no one to turn to in her moment of crisis.

The woman would say, "There are so many women like you who could take these babies and do a wonderful job as a mother."

I didn't condone abusive behavior, but a small part of me felt sorry for those women who had a tough time. It was always the moms with the easy kids who were horrified by these incidents. They both needed help.

My insight worked better in my youth; my brain wasn't filled with the useless information that came with age. Now that I had a son of my own, insight was more difficult. There were times when I started to think that I was on the verge of observing a connection between Rocky's biting (sometimes even drawing blood from playmates) and his out-of-control crying and the ingestion of certain foods, medicines, and environmental elements. When Rocky was young, most people didn't make a connection between Rocky's behaviors and the bright-colored fruity cereals or the neon vitamins and flavored medicines we gave him.

◆ ◆ ◆

On Rocky's first Halloween night, the red wooden wagon was readied and waiting on my front steps. My neighbor, who also had a boy around Rocky's age, came down to our house so that we could take our kids trick-or-treating around a few blocks to show them off. Rocky and his friend Eric were going as cowboys. They sat one behind the other. The mothers eagerly flashed cameras before starting out in order to immortalize their first Halloween moments as bogus cowboys.

Even at such a young age, they knew something exciting was going to happen. As we approached each pumpkin-lit house, neighbors would come to their doors, and the two idiot mothers would say, "Trick or treat," in unison. The kids, who were now hatless and working on ridding themselves of their cowboy neck scarves, didn't even look up. As we started opening the bags and they spied the candy, they caught on. At the third house, they suddenly morphed into eager puppies waiting for a treat, unable to sit still.

After only one short street, we turned the corner and witnessed Rocky throwing up all over his plaid shirt. I tried to pry the Tootsie Pop from his hand while he held onto it with unbelievable strength, as he knew instinctively it was the last of his candy. This was fun. He was screaming, and I was pulling his hands apart. I was sure my friend wished she had her own wagon by now. I took Rocky's scarf and wiped him up as best as I could.

"Oh, it's OK," I said. "We can continue down another street. He'll be OK; don't worry. I just won't let him have any more candy."

"Are you sure, Vicky?"

"Yeah, it's OK. He's thrown up before."

I should have gone home, but I didn't want to miss out on the social interaction with the neighborhood. I didn't want to be left out.

As Rocky caught his breath, he started to scream for his candy. I looked at him, looked at my friend and the street ahead, and reached in the bag and pulled out the plainest piece of candy I could find in order to quiet him. He settled down. We continued down the street, but our hearts weren't in it anymore. I knew I did the wrong thing by giving into Rocky. At the time, I had no idea how bad it was for him. I never realized how fragile his body chemistry was, especially since I didn't know any other children with problems like his. We were surrounded by healthy children of all ages.

You can tell if kids have allergies if they have runny noses, but what about those crabby children who don't have runny noses but who constantly have behavior problems at home or in school? Sometimes these kids are wrongly diagnosed with attention deficit hyperactivity disorder. I was told repeatedly that Rocky's actions couldn't possibly be due to allergies.

I saw that if Rocky ate certain baby foods or treats, he would start to scream or throw up. But it was never consistent enough to give me an aha moment. If I mentioned this to other mothers, they would say, "Oh, sometimes things disagree with Bobby, too. Maybe Rocky is getting teeth early."

I knew deep down that it wasn't his teeth; it was something more serious, and no one would listen to me. I visited bookstore after bookstore. I read every index in every health, allergy, and asthma book and looked for a clue. There was nothing about behavior and artificial flavors or food colors, and personal computers were not around for Googling yet.

Another holiday was approaching: Christmas. It was time to select our first live tree. I made sure that Rocky was dressed in his red-plaid flannel shirt and little prefaded jeans from the Gap for that special photo-op moment. Yes, he was an adorable boy, as he held Daddy's hand and strolled through the Black Forest to pick the perfect tree for our home. Who cared if this Black Forest was across from Target and Mervyns? We didn't let a little thing like lack of snow, eighty-degree weather, and sweat running down our foreheads to ruin this memorable moment. We were standing, camera loaded, in a parking lot, next to the 405 Freeway.

As my dad used to say, "A guy can make what he wants out of life."

A few days later as I hung the final ornament—bang! We had an emergency asthma attack. I rushed to the hospital. Steve was away on a short trip, so when I returned home, I called my neighbor Deane to come over and take the tree outside. He was a single guy we used to go out with a lot and probably had been the most surprised of all the neighbors when we'd brought a baby home.

"Where do you want me to put the tree?" he said, trying to help a tired friend.

"Maybe it isn't the tree. Maybe we should wait and see." I couldn't think clearly from lack of sleep.

"Okay," he said, hoisting it up and setting it back in the corner.

"No, take it out. I can't take a chance; it must be the pine needles that started his attack. It's just that he was so excited about the tree and I worked so hard on it and it's so beautiful. Rocky and Steve picked it out together."

"Vic, we could leave it until tomorrow," he said.

"No, better not take any chances. We don't want to go back to the hospital...What do you think I should do?"

"Maybe we should take it out, and you could see if he gets better," he said, gripping the trunk through the decorated branches.

"All right. I guess that's a good idea. I just can't think."

Out it went.

On Steve's return, he walked in and saw the decorated tree through the French doors. I told him of the rotating tree incident, and he was dumbfounded how even a simple holiday could be turned upside down in the matter of a few days. He was sorry he had been away and unavailable to help me with the hospital or the tree. Leaving the job to our neighbor was not something he embraced as a father or a husband.

◆ ◆ ◆

Kind neighbors would listen to my story once, maybe twice, but more than that was pushing it. I was obsessive and boring as I tried to figure out Rocky's problems with anyone who would listen. I know now that many of these conversations were self-promoting.

I needed to assure everyone that I had been the corporate woman who stood for solutions; I had the fast sports car and trips to Europe. I was the one people called upon in the world of corporate emergencies. Now I looked forward to talking with anyone over three feet high. I was not the broken-down mother they saw before them; my babbling was not the sign of an inept individual. I was a college graduate, for God's sake!

"Just checking your water meter today. How ya doin?" said the young meter lady.

"Oh, just trying to catch up on my wash. Did you know that bananas stain baby clothes?"

"Wow, that's terrible," she said, with her head stuck in our meter box.

"Yeah. I've ruined two great outfits already."

"OK, then. Take care. Hope you get those stains out."

"See you," I said.

What was happening to me? I was scaring myself with this wild banter. Embarrassed, I backed into the house.

The next morning the phone rang and jolted me back to reality. It was a nutritionist calling. A friend had suggested I contact her. She asked me to sum up Rocky's problems. My mouth was jump-started by the caffeine I had been enjoying. I tried to paint her a picture.

"When did you notice his health problems getting out of hand?"

I told her that from the beginning, they had flowed together like an Alaskan oil spill, overlapping and seeping in all around me. Now eighteen months had passed.

"I hope you can help me," I said. "I've been to every kind of doctor. I feel I need a combination of doctors, but no one will address this issue with me. Everyone keeps to his or her own domain."

"Don't worry; I won't leave you alone with this problem," she said. "I will stick with you until your son is better."

It was like Oprah herself was handling my case. I did not even care if what she said was true. I was ready to live with false hope.

The nutritionist taught us what additives to watch out for and how to eat in a more natural way. We learned which crops received the most pesticides, such as the peanuts in peanut butter and raisins. She taught me to use natural peanut butters and natural cereals, not the eye-popping, colored ones with artificial dyes.

She suggested I start shopping at Mother's health store in Newport Beach. In the snack aisle, I reached over a short hippie-type guy with many body piercings and a skinny brown ponytail. I grabbed some natural cookies I thought Rocky might like because they were shaped like the regular animal cookies. They had no preservatives or artificial colors. Holding my new find, I glanced around at the clientele. There seemed to be three types of clientele. Old hippies who wore their Birkenstocks with deflated socks resting like sleeping rattlers around their ankles. The younger hippies who had no need for socks but liked body piercing. The new-money moms, who strutted around in tight Nike workout clothes, doing squats while selecting organic bananas.

Well, when I got this new food, Rocky would start to feel better and we would get more sleep, and then I would have more energy to dress nicely, have my hair done, and grab life with gusto. I could return to my old self, go out on a date with my husband, tell jokes, and maybe even have friends over for dinner. It's amazing that my hope never faded during those times. I wasn't raised to think there was a better tomorrow, but it's funny how I could be at the bottom of the barrel and maintain faith that all would work out. Faith was never tested when everything was running smoothly—big surprise, I know. Faith had to do with supreme trust that through rough times, God would take care of me. He put Rocky, Steve, and me together for a reason. Maybe he had a sense of humor like me and knew I could handle it. All I could say was, "Ha-ha, God, very funny."

Continuing on my journey, I hit all the snack rows and threw in natural corn curls, baked chips, wheatless crackers, cereal that looked like bad cereal but wasn't, no-nitrate hot dogs, and natural-juice Popsicles with great abandonment. I thought my problems were solved. At the last minute, I picked up some natural candy. Life was going to be OK now. Why hadn't I thought of this store before? This would be more expense and more work, but with a little discipline, we would do well. My friend Christine shopped here. She read everything on everything and was a doctor's worst nightmare—always questioning when something wasn't clear. Something more people should do. Her kids were basically healthy and happy, which gave her the upper hand over my situation.

I had to explain Rocky's diet of the week to mothers and friends when he went somewhere. Some people, especially older neighbors, thought it was too silly. What he needed was tried and true medicines and discipline, nothing else. It had worked for their kids, for God's sake.

The health food helped some, but nothing made a significant difference. Our nutritionist helped, but not as we had planned. She sent me to the nutritionist who had trained her years before. "I think your son's behavior is due to low blood sugar. Make sure he stops for a snack midmorning and midafternoon," said the older nutritionist. Great, a new theory.

Each time we had a good day, I would think, *Yes, this is it; the start of a new way of life with our son.* We would trek out to the swings and slides in our neighborhood for a half hour or so and then come back in for a grilled-cheese lunch with applesauce. He loved to chat and ask questions about all sorts of things, as if he were at a luncheon with friends at the club. "Why does the cheese stick to the bread? Do bears dream?"

On those days after the third reading of *Puppy on the Farm* and a short nap, we would head back to the kitchen for finger painting—if you can call it that. Talking away, Rocky would climb up on a stool, take a huge glob of paint, and, using his arm like a squeegee, push it across the white tile counter. This ensured him a chance to get into the sink to wash up. After fifteen minutes of art, he was ready for the real goal of painting. I pulled a chair up to the sink, and he washed his arms and the same plates and pots over and over again, turning the water on and off constantly while singing his own combo of songs: "A little dog lives on my street. Bow, wow, wow. The farmer's in the dell, and he went ring round the rosy..."

But a good day could easily be it followed by an asthma day, where he would get so frustrated with his health. Most mothers would complain if they had one bad day with their child; our life was the opposite. We truthfully looked forward to the good moments and days, and we took full advantage of them with playdates under blanket tents, picnics at parks, and wagon rides around our neighborhood, when he would wave to everyone while holding his baby pillow with chew marks.

It was a Monday morning, and there sat Rocky and I in another cheaply decorated office of brown plastic furniture and old magazines. This time it was an office in Huntington Beach. We waited and waited for the new doctor who was supposed to help us and who, like the other nutritionists, didn't take insurance. I filled out forms, and Rocky played with old broken blocks. After I finished the paper work, I pulled him on my lap and gave him a big hug, kisses, and tickles. We both sat with anticipation.

"The doctor will see you now."

There was something about this place that gave me the creeps, but I suppressed those thoughts and decided to hang on to enough hope for the two of us.

The doctor had an arrogant attitude, but I was willing to be humble if it helped my son. As she glanced over our chart, she said, "You should not be giving this child soy milk; he is too allergic. Here is the name of a nondairy product with no milk or soy. This is what he should be on. It is in the supermarket by the regular milk. No wonder he is having problems."

"Are you sure this is good for him?" I asked. "He doesn't do well with artificial products. You should see what happened to him when I gave him a little nondairy dessert topping. He couldn't stop vomiting. It was frightening."

"I am sure you will be surprised by the results. Let me know how he is doing in a week."

I had a feeling it wouldn't work. Wasn't there a lot of artificial stuff in that phony milk product? I hoped I was wrong. She had studied in China with supposedly the best doctors. The next day after a few sips of the nondairy drink, Rocky started to vomit uncontrollably. Holding Rocky over the bathtub with a towel, I called the doctor, the phone cradling my neck.

"My son is very ill from the milk product you suggested. What should I do? He can't stop throwing up."

"What was your name again?" asked the doctor.

We had a pediatrician who was wonderful and caring as long as I didn't question his years of experience. Every time I would bring up the subject of additives and allergies, he would sigh and give me "the look" with a smile, as if to say, "Mercy me, all you new mothers are alike, aren't you?" I seemed to constantly run into doctors who enjoyed making me feel stupid. I wasn't stupid. I was smart, and this smart woman was going to find another doctor with more experience in the field. Mothers of sick kids are not try-ing to be special and garner attention; we need serious help and need to be taken seriously.

We continued with our old system of watching out for triggers. We were tired of mauve waiting rooms with stain-resistant carpet, green hospital walls, cold floors, and cheap artwork. We tried to have a normal family life.

On Sundays, we'd head for the old Irvine County Park. After breakfast, we would load the car with the Sunday papers, books, magazines, soft drinks, water, folding chairs, blankets, snacks, and video cameras. Then we would start on the Rocky stuff: drinks, flannel cowboy blanket, snacks, bright-colored play toys, his favorite pillow with the corner sucked off, a stuffy animal, sun screen, and a change of clothes.

Trying to get Rocky to sleep, Steve and I then drove around for about an hour or longer. Rocky was still having trouble grasping the concept of sleeping through the night. These trips started when he was about three months old and continued most Sundays for years. A loop was the best route. That way, if he fell asleep, we were pointed toward the park or home and not San Diego, which would enable us to relax before he woke up. As soon as his eyes started to bob up and down, we, the take-charge parents, were crossing the park entrance gate. As we pulled up to the ticket booth, the parking attendant would glance in and bellow, "So how you doin' this bright and beautiful day?"

His booming, cheery voice would make us recoil and push our bodies against the seats, a physical reaction to the possibility of Rocky waking up. That would mean all our driving gone to waste and no Sunday reading under a shady tree or people watching as we rested in the serene grove of towering trees.

We answered back in a tense, hushed tone, "Fine, thank you." Steve handed him two dollars, and off we went, careful not to rush over the grate at the entrance. We unknowingly held our breaths as we rode over the first tire bump and then the second. We looked back to see if Rocky had moved. His head shifted to the right; his eyes fluttered. I took a deep breath and held it, waiting, but he was only fooling us in his sleep.

Turning left, we drove to the back of the park and the sycamore trees with their mottled gray bark that had stood there together for over a hundred years. We passed all the hand-printed signs attached to posts saying, "Newton family reunion," "Canter company picnic," or "Maria's first birthday." Many signs were adorned with balloons taped around them—some ripe for popping, others hanging like damp socks. The back of the park was my favorite area, wild and remote and away from all the barbecues, worn playground equipment, and radios. Steve would ease the car into a user-friendly, tree-filled area, and we, like midnight thieves, would slowly, oh-so slowly, open the car doors. They would remain cracked open a few inches as we read the *New York Times* under the canopy of leaves and listened to the birds and chattering squirrels until Rocky woke up.

At this park, no one seemed to worry about eating or wearing oversized shorts, as they did in Newport Beach. One picnicker sat in a folding chair and ate a giant sub sandwich. When he got up, his chair went with him, like a giant clamshell shutting up from fear. I started to laugh aloud but quickly covered my mouth for fear of waking Rocky. This park was my favorite. Families were having softball games or pushing kids on swings. It just seemed simpler here, where no one knew you, away from the beach cities and the fast lanes of everyday.

When Rocky woke up, which was fairly soon, we took him out of the car, walked him around the grounds for about thirty minutes, and then headed over to the small zoo on the property.

We took him to see the "wild beasts," like pigs, cows, and chickens. We stuck a stack of quarters in the chicken gumball machine that doled out a handful of ground-up corn and then threw feed out, trying to lure the creatures closer. So many families had thrown feed out all day that the chickens, even if hit in the head, would not blink. When we all had had enough, we headed back to the car and started the arduous job of repacking for the drive home. It took us an hour to get there by our special nap-time route and ten minutes to get home with Rocky wide awake. I didn't realize then that all the animal dander, feathers, and dust were poison for any allergic person, especially a little person with tiny airways. I thought it was mostly food allergies. Sometimes he would get agitated when we left, but we just thought he was being stubborn. If he got asthma later on in the day, we never put it together because of the time span.

One Sunday afternoon we came home to our usual Sunday neighbor guests, who liked to gather on our porch for their weekend cocktails. We lived in a new, "perfectly planned" community called Irvine, near Newport Beach. We joked and called it "Irvana." This, basically, was the first big house for everyone, so each neighbor made an effort to be social. Many friends would bring snacks over, and we would provide the drinks. The adults could chat while the older children played and took care of the smaller ones. It was a relief for us not to have our eyes rotating back and forth as if we were searchlights at San Quentin. Someone else's child always played with our kid.

One time as I was coming outside with a plate of cheese and crackers, I heard Rocky scream, "Cookie!"

"Rocky, that cookie is very bad for you. Here, take this pretty cracker."

"No, cookie!"

"Why did you bring those cookies out here? You know that if Rocky eats one, he'll act up," I screamed quietly through my teeth to Steve.

"I didn't bring them out; the neighbor brought them over," Steve said sharply.

All the neighbors were watching us. Since the Bateses had become a family, people watched less afternoon sports and soaps; we were much more entertaining.

"Hurry, kids; you can finish your homework later. The Bateses will be coming out soon. We have to get down there."

All eyes fixed on two-year-old Rocky as he started to run around. Fueled by the ingredients in the cookie, he headed for our sidewalk to bang his head. I scooped him up quickly. With only seconds left on the clock and a glass of white wine in my free hand, I was going for a touchdown. The crowd held its breath. With Rocky's body tightly secured under my left arm, I swiftly ran in and out of tricycles and skateboards with one goal in mind. I could feel the anticipating looks of approval and awe. I headed straight for the grass, sideswiped a yellow Lab at the last minute, and set Rocky down in the soft grass.

Feeling sure that I had rescued him from deliberately cracking his head on the sidewalk, I turned to my friends. As I gazed over at neighbors in triumph, I noticed their eyes shifting past me. There was Rocky behind me, clumsily running at lightning speed, back to the sidewalk. I was too old for this shit. Someone was going to do some changing here. I would break him of this. As soon as I got some sleep, I would start. Did I mention how smart he was, how beautiful he was…that through all of this I loved him passion- ately, completely, so deeply that it was beyond words?

When I couldn't handle Rocky's crying and uneasiness, I would head for the beach or the tub. Water always soothed him, like the effects of tranquilizer-dart gun I coveted from the *Wild Animal Kingdom* show.

He had no fear of the roaring ocean waves or the pool. I can't even think of anything that scared him. He had daredevil blood in him and wanted to experience all life offered as quickly as possible. Once at our neighborhood pool, someone yelled, "Your son jumped in the water!"

He had walked over to the grassy play area as I was locating a chair to sit down in. Next thing I knew, I was leaping into the pool to retrieve him. As I climbed out of the water, my beige silk pants were embarrassingly glued to my thighs. Rocky grabbed my neck and smiled. "Mommy swimming, too?" It was a big joke to him.

We would play around water as often as we could because it was such a pleasure for all of us. Many times if Steve were traveling, I would drive Rocky down to Laguna Beach for a picnic. There we fought off sea gulls for our lunch and laughed as they took Rocky's bag of potato chips and flew away. He would put his hands on his tiny hips and, with authority, look up and yell, "Hey, you guys! Bring my chips back. I told them, Mommy."

We would wait our turn for the swings or look for shells or rocks along the shore, and then when we were tired of playing in the ocean, we'd pack up and walk back to the car through the nearby toy store, where we would slowly investigate every aisle. Once we sat for over a half hour eating an ice cream cone and watching a large crane knock down an old building; he always had patience to do things like that.

Years later when we went to Old Faithful in Yellowstone with another family, Rocky would walk out to a small geyser hole by himself and sit waiting for the water to shoot upward. The other kids would get bored and run back to Old Faithful or play tag, but he just sat there and waited for as long as it took, like an old man with nothing better to do. Everything was interesting to him. His favorite line was "I didn't know that!" when we answered some unusual question for him.

On the way home from Laguna Beach, he would sleep with the window cracked open, his naturally tanned legs flopped open, heading for dreamland.

Rocky could play in the bathtub for an entire evening, after which he should have slept well. Our bathroom had a large, open, sunken tub that was perfect as a wading kiddy pool. It seemed like only yesterday that my husband and I had sat in there with a glass wine. Now plastic buckets, Rocky, and trolls occupied it.

The routine was always the same. Start the tub, get out my $12.99 blue-plastic banana chaise, unfold it next to the tub, grab a magazine, strip Rocky, add the toys, test the water, add the kid, and then ease into my lounge chair with a deep sigh of relief.

"Mommy, I need Mr. Kitty."

"In a minute, Rocky. Mommy just sat down."

"Now, Mommy. Mr. Kitty dirty."

Sighing, I would struggle out of the wobbly banana chaise, pull him out of the tub, and try to find Mr. Kitty. Of course I wouldn't be able to locate the dumb kitty and would run back.

He would be singing, "A little kitty lives on my street, meow, meow, meow."

"Rocky, Mr. Kitty says he wants to sleep now. He says Rocky should sleep more."

"Mr. Kitty is sleeping now?"

What, are you deaf? I would ease back down to the horizontal position. I'd grab my wet magazine, full of beautiful, single, *Vogue* models, and look hard at him with a practiced closed-lip smile.

"Wash the trolls."

After an hour or more, I would take him out. He might have shrunk a diaper size, but he seemed relaxed.

◆ ◆ ◆

I started to wonder how my mother had done it. Having two kids and no assistance from my father, she must have always been running on empty.

When you grow up in an alcoholic family, as I did, you watch shows like *Father Knows Best* and think that's how the neighbors really live. Children from "normal" homes know that the perfect Anderson TV family—Kitten, Bud, and Kathy with the mother always smiling and never a hair out of place—was a fraud. Life seemed simpler in black and white.

An alcoholic doesn't have problems. If our dad had a bad day, he would drink. Problem solved. He felt entitled. If my mother had one of her frequent migraine headaches, she still had to take care of us kids, cook dinner, and worry about her husband and his whereabouts at all hours.

Our mother was always treading stormy waters. It was as if she were stretched out over the turbulent waves each day and dogpaddling relentlessly trying to keep her head above water. It was hard to stay afloat when a family was tugging at you. She knew that at any minute, she could be pulled under from a marriage of exhaustion, anger, and tension, all of which filtered down to the children. We unknowingly embraced those emotions and filed them for future families. We didn't understand the lack of affection. We were baby birds who could never get enough.

Only after becoming a mother with a difficult child did I finally understand my mom's life and forgive her for the lack of attention during my early years. I realized that she loved me as best as she could while she struggled with her marriage and health. She did all she could do. We became closer as I experienced my own difficulties and self-doubts as a mother.

Chapter Eight

I decided to take Rocky home to see my folks. It's a trip forever etched on my mind.

I was getting situated in my plane seat, and I was quite nervous. This was my first plane ride with Rocky to see the relatives. Luckily my friend Sue was on the same plane; she was connecting in Salt Lake City and going on with her two young boys to Wisconsin after our stop in Chicago. Seeing her across the aisle made me take a sigh of relief.

"Are you all set up over there?" Sue said with a smile.

"I think so." I gave a nervous laugh.

Just as we became airborne, Rocky started to vomit up the hot dog he'd had at the airport in a lovely projectile fashion. As I held him up under his arms, not knowing which way to turn him, I glanced up and saw the seat-belt sign. The crowning achievement was that he not only targeted his own airplane outfit with vomit but also the gentleman's arm next to me. And yes, my friends, that is how you get two empty seats next to you when flying across the country. Later in the flight, he decided to scream during the movie, which caused all the passengers to shift in their seats.

Sue asked if she could help while her two Gerber-baby boys were humming to themselves and coloring. Was it karmic payback for all those pre-child trips I had taken when I'd said, "Can't those people keep those babies quiet?" Finally the answer came to me. No, they cannot.

The stay with Grandma was uneventful, unless you count the trip to the emergency room at one in the morning during a severe Chicago lightning storm. Coughing, Rocky woke me up. His shoulders started pulling up hard, and I knew we needed to get to the local hospital quickly.

I can still hear my mom saying, "Can't we wait until it stops raining?"

Oh my God. Did they not understand that he could die?

The next evening I was sitting in my dad's living room, and I casually told him we were adopting a second child. My dad's face went blank. His blue eyes opened wide on his weathered face, and his mouth dropped open. He proceeded to give me a few meaningful words of advice, just like the old days: "Are you crazy? Haven't you had enough trouble already?"

There I sat. I was the little girl again, sharing a room with a man who still could push my buttons. I could feel that old searing tightness in my chest from childhood coming back. How could an accomplished adult still have her buttons pushed by her parents? I said, "Dad, you told us before not to mess with our 'perfect' lives and adopt the first time."

He said, "And wasn't I right?"

That hurt. I know that he was trying to protect me that he had suffered along with us through many of Rock's illnesses but he would never get it. How could anyone from the outside know that even though it was a hard journey, Rocky filled our hearts with love? We thought that giving him a brother or sister would bring balance to him, and since we were older parents, Rocky would have a sibling to share and grow with.

To tell the truth, we thought getting our first baby so fast was a fluke. We'd been told it usually took about a year. So we thought it wouldn't hurt to talk to our lawyer and get our name on the list. We could always change our minds. We had time.

"Are you sure you want to do this? You know I have to travel a lot, which puts a larger burden on you," Steve said, truly concerned for me.

"I think it would be good for us all. Another baby couldn't possibly be as hard as Rocky," I replied. "Let's at least talk to the lawyer."

"Well, we can talk with him, but let's not make a firm commitment until we take a harder look at this."

"Okay, good idea," I said.

After our meeting with the lawyer, we drove home in silence, both in deep thought laced with doubt. Why were we inviting more sleepless nights, more crying, and more stress? What if he or she turned out to have problems similar to Rocky's? What if the problems were worse?

Were we on a spiritual journey with these babies? Or as my dear father would say, was it trip to the nuthouse?

Would a second child push us over the edge? Was it a brilliant idea or sheer madness? Who was to say that the idea of adding a new little human being to our family was right or wrong? As in any adoption, there always was a sense of the unknown; you had to emotionally get around that issue. I knew couples that were interested in adoption and longed for a baby but had commitment fears. They wouldn't even take the first step to investigate the process; it was too daunting for them even though they constantly thought about doing it.

Rocky was three years old when we adopted a second child, and it was then that we started to see the light. Our new son, Jackson, went with the flow and knew how to float. He slept easily and cried very little. When we attended to him, the reward was a welcoming, content look.

Deciding to have Jackson was the best thing we ever did; it was pure genius. If people thought us silly to adopt another child, they quickly changed their minds upon seeing our new shining star.

The call came in a month. Surprise! Special delivery for the Bates family. A woman had changed her mind about keeping her baby, and it was due any day. We sure had some gift for getting kids! I told our lawyer that Steve was coming in late from a long business trip. Did we have to come up that night (over a two-hour drive) to meet the birth mother?

"Can't it wait one day?" I said.

He said, "If you can't come up, it's okay; I will just take the next couple on the list. There will be other chances."

I can't explain it, but when he told me that the birth mother was a Filipina and the father was of Italian decent and a chemist, I thought of Rocky, who was Nicaraguan and Italian. This baby seemed so right to me. I was anxiously in love.

We made the trip to LA. The lawyer suggested we meet at a Japanese steak house, where they cook the food in front of you. As Steve and I walked in, the lawyer, the birth mother, and her boyfriend were already sitting down. This was a new experience, meeting and talking with the birth mother first, in person. Our lawyer was certainly not a Chatty Cathy, so Steve and I had to be on our toes and keep the conversation flowing. We were very nervous. She was small and very pregnant. I couldn't read the menu without my glasses, but I didn't want to put them on for fear she would think me too old to raise her baby.

She ordered, and I said, "That sounds great. I'll have that, too."

Applying my theory of two birds with one stone: food and kissing up. She was so calm and confident; would it rub off on the baby? She said she was Catholic and that was one reason she picked us. Boy, I had better start brushing up. All those years in Catholic school were finally paying off! We left the restaurant feeling confident that all would go smoothly.

The hospital she chose, which we visited four times, was two hours from our house on the other side of Los Angeles.

"She's in labor; get up as soon as you can," the lawyer would say.

We would run around, get a sitter, gas up the car, and head up to the valley, north of Los Angeles. It was always a false alarm.

When we came back home, Rocky would say, "Where's my baby?"

"Not yet, Rocky. Maybe next week, buddy," Steve would say.

Rocky was waiting for us and ready for introductions.

Finally on Sunday night, we were all in bed watching television. I had been staring at some elephant peeling bark off a tree for about ten minutes when the phone rang. Rocky was just dozing off; in fact, we all were.

"This is it. The baby is coming. She's in labor," said the lawyer.

Steve looked at me. "I'll better stay with Rocky. We can't get a sitter at this late moment, and besides, it's probably another false alarm."

Why did these babies always come on their own schedule? I kissed everyone good-bye, and away I journeyed, alone with my own thoughts. In the darkened car, among all the 405 Freeway traffic heading north, I felt isolated. Everyone was going somewhere in a hurry. Was this really the moment? How would our family change with a new baby? Would we have problems with the birth mother? She didn't have my phone number. Whenever she wanted to talk with me during the pregnancy, she would call our lawyer, and he would contact me to call her. We'd had no contact with the previous birth mother, and at times, it felt uncomfortable just talking to her. Then one day she called and told me she had gone to a psychic.

"I walked into this woman's office and sat down," she said. "I had never seen her before. She looked at me and said, 'You're making the right decision, giving your baby up to that family; they will be good parents.' I couldn't believe that she told me that, but I know you will be a good mother."

"Thank you," I said. What if the woman had said we would be terrible parents? I had to reassure myself that there was a divine plan and that this baby was part of our journey.

When I arrived at the hospital, our lawyer greeted me and took me to the waiting area. Later I was directed to the dimly lit room, and there was the birth mother on her side, moaning from labor pains.

This was not the time for perky conversation and telling her about the extremely heavy traffic coming up. I was tired, but no one could accuse me of not reading a room. As she kept moaning, I tightly crossed and corkscrewed my legs around me. This was a natural reaction by any woman who hadn't had a baby. Her eyes rolled toward me and then closed as another pain shot through her body. I wondered how long this labor thing would take. It looked painful. Birth mothers should consider an hourly rate. Just then the doctor came in and checked her.

"Are you the adoptive mother-to-be?"

"Yes."

"Well, you should go get some rest. There is nothing you can do here, and this baby is not coming until morning. If something happens, we'll call you. Leave a number."

The only nearby motel was in a remote location and was used mainly for army personnel. I got directions and headed across the freeway. I was dead tired from a day with Rocky. The stress of the adoption process combined with no sleep, the long drive, and having to interact with strangers was taking its toll. Once there, I had to be alert and attentive and project my best to everyone. I didn't want them to change their minds about giving us a baby. My neck muscles were tightening, and I was gearing up for a major headache. It was all so overwhelming to me.

I parked by the dimly lit office and registered. Once I received the room key, I drove around to the back with my car doors locked. Checking all around, I ran out and unlocked the room. It smelled of smoke and parties. I immediately pulled down the bedspread, lay down on the rumpled sheets, and passed out. At four in the morning, I had slept only a few hours, but something told me to get back to the hospital. Reversing the process, I peeked out the window at the dark parking lot. There was only one old car in the corner of the lot. I adjusted my car keys in my hand, ran, and jumped into my car; locking the doors, I headed out across the freeway. I took a deep breath and thought that soon we would be a family of four. When I entered the labor room, it was empty. A nurse approached me.

"Are you the adoptive mother?"

"Yes, has the baby been born yet? I was supposed to be in the room with the delivery. No one called me."

"It happened quickly. It was a caesarian, so you couldn't have been in the room. But you have a healthy baby boy. Congratulations."

"Can I see him?"

"First you need to talk to Social Services and show them some identification. Then they will contact us with the okay."

I quickly walked down to Social Services and back, and then, sashaying toward me, came the nurse with a bundle of baby and a smile.

"Here is your new son."

I reached out, and she placed him in the cradle my arms provided. He was only a few hours old, and when I said, "Hi," he opened his eyes and looked right at me as if to say, "What took you so long? I've been waiting for you my whole life."

I was in love and cried.

Jackson had to stay in the hospital for a few days because the mother had been on an antibiotic. Each day I would drive up and spend time rocking and singing to him "I Love My Baby (My Baby Loves Me)."

He opened his eyes and looked up at me, as if trying to figure out where the noise was coming from.

When I went to visit the birth mother, she said, "It's time I went back to school and work. It will be good if my son is raised in a nice suburban home. It is the right thing to do for him."

On the day I was to take Jackson home, I went into the birth mother's room to say good-bye.

"Will you walk down to the nursery to see the baby with me?" she said. "I would like to hold him once before you leave."

Every day God gave me a chance for spiritual growth and said, "I know you can deal with this, Vicky," easy for him to say. I took a deep breath.

I watched as the nurse gently placed the baby in her arms. She sat in the same rocker I had sat in for the last few days. The nurses and I silently looked on behind a glass window and wondered if she would change her mind. She looked at him so tenderly and placed her hand on his soft, downy hair and paused for a minute. After a few minutes, she stood up and walked toward us and handed Jackson to me.

It took a brave woman to give her baby up. It would only take one word to take him back.

"Well, I wish you good luck. I hope things go well for you and your family. I'm sure he will be a good baby," she said, getting up casually.

"You, too. I will love and cherish your child," I said, with thankful relief.

Unless the mother changed her mind at the court hearing, he was our baby son now. Rocky got the new brother he had wished, waited, and prayed for so patiently.

Downstairs, Steve had checked us out, and we were ready to head home to show Jackson his big brother, Rocky.

The moment we brought Jackson home and put him in Rocky's lap, the whole family lit up. Rocky was so excited about having a new brother; he immediately planned to show his new play object all the ropes.

"Mommy, I can take care of my brother. Can I take him to the park? I could put him in my wagon and go show Kurtie, OK?"

Rocky peered up at us with a great big smile, while his tiny hand tried to pat the top of Jackson's black punk-rock baby hair.

"Rocky, I think he is a little tired. You know it's a lot of work being born. I know you will make a great big brother. Look how he's looking at you already. He must really like you."

What I really wanted to say was, "Rocky, you're a natural. Mommy will be back to check in on you in a few hours after she has had a hot bath and a glass of merlot."

I was emotionally and physically drained again.

Our new family member was so calm we couldn't believe it. He was a special blessing. Jackson built up our poor self-image as parents and took some attention off of Number One Son. When I scan his baby book today, almost every page reads, "Jackson is so happy, so easy."

He delighted in playing with others, sitting by himself, or being used as a Toys R Us product by his brother. Nothing fazed him. He was always the eye in any family storm, calm and watchful. After Jackson started saying the basic "mommy" and "daddy" words, he started talking about his big brother.

I had just picked up my beloved mail, which had everything for the housebound—catalogues, politics, book reviews, bring it all on. I grabbed a diet Coke, put my feet up on the sofa and my down throw pillow behind my back. I was living. It was scary how little it took to entertain me now. I was involved in an article when I spied a Baby Gap ad on the adjacent page. That's when the thought dawned on me. *Babies? I have those. Where the heck are they, and what are they up to?* It had been so quiet. And you know what that means. As I walked down the hallway, no sound was coming from their room. When I turned the corner, I heard small noises from under Jackson's crib.

Bending down on my knees, I said, "Guys, what are you two doing under there?"

"Look," Rocky said, crawling out from under the bed frame with his brother.

Rocky had just given Jackson a haircut with his Mommy and Me scissors. There across Jackson's straight-cut baby bangs was a two-inch missing square, like a jack-o'-lantern mouth with a missing tooth.

With pride and a huge smile, Jackson peeked his head out at me from under the crib and added three new words, "Wockey dude it."

That week I had had a portrait scheduled with a photo studio that was difficult to get into; the appointment would have to be changed. I had learned early on about photo shoots with Rocky, what to do and what to avoid. When Rocky was first born, a neighbor of mine with a baby boy the same age suggested we go down to Sears.

"They have a special on baby photos. You get a whole bunch for nineteen ninety-five, so what can you lose? We'll go after dinner."

"I don't know about Sears. How good can it be?"

"It's nineteen ninety-five. Who cares?"

Since I was not into the bunny-rabbit pastel scene, I dressed Rocky in a navy turtleneck and khaki baby pants. A week later we went to pick up our pictures.

"Gee, they're a little dark," my friend said, as she opened the envelope and peeked at her photos. If her kid, who looked like an albino, was dark, I needed to see my pictures right away. As I was driving, she handed me my envelope.

"Here, you open it," I said, afraid to look, and handed them back.

At the next stoplight, I glanced over as she held them up to me.

"Oh my God, a little dark? He looks like Michael Jackson. You can't tell where his turtleneck ends and his head begins. Give me those pictures. All he needs is a record deal. This isn't worth it even if they were free. It doesn't even look like him, does it?"

"The lighting was bad in there. You could try again with a lighter shirt," she said, obviously trying to make me feel better.

"You're kidding, right?"

Immediately I vowed to find a proper studio that knew how to light small children, no matter what the price. Who knew? There were so many hidden pressures for a mother.

♦ ♦ ♦

At one and one-half years old, Jackson was admitted to the hospital with bronchitis. The day before, Steve had been called away on business, so I got a sitter for Rocky and stayed in the hospital with Jackson. After all the problems with Rocky, the doctors were not taking any chances. The signal that a child has asthma can vary from colds that hang on forever to constant coughing at night when they are put to bed. Many parents are unaware their kids even have asthma and think every day that they'll get better. After all the time I had spent in the hospital watching Rocky through the nights, I wasn't going to take any chances with Jackson.

How could I help Jackson when I had so few family health details to go on because of the adoption? A little voice inside me said this couldn't be a repeat of Rocky's health patterns. If it was, how could I ever go through it again? The boys weren't blood related, so how could this be? For some reason, there is a high instance of asthma in adopted children. Does a mother's stress during pregnancy, as she thinks about adoption, affect the lung development or add to the chance the child will develop asthma later?

Even though he was sick in the hospital, there was Jackson at two in the morning, pushing a little grocery cart around the halls in his fuzzy, plastic blue-footed pajamas. His stick-straight hair was up and unbending, as if it were spray starched. He kept circling the floor, exchanging smiles with all the nurses. Each time around, they would fill his cart with cotton balls and tiny juices and official-looking papers. Always Mr. Happy.

That evening I saw a woman pulling a red flexible flyer wagon around the same floors. In it laid a little girl about Jackson's age. After we passed each other a few times, I asked what had happened to her child. She told me she had twin girls and that both had been admitted for severe flu the previous week. The curly-haired girl I was looking at had received the wrong IV and was now paralyzed. Why are we targeted with these traumas? I would have insight years later.

I read in some hospital medical report that "Children who were seen between 4:00 a.m. and 8:00 a.m., children who were treated for severe diseases, and children seen on weekends were at higher risk for prescribing errors. In addition, trainees were more likely to make medication errors than staff physicians."

All the nights I had stayed up with Rocky in the hospital helped me understand how tired and overworked nurses and doctors could be. No human is sharp at three in the morning. I would never leave my child alone in the hospital.

Jackson only stayed the one night, and I was relieved to know that it was not likely he would follow in Rocky's footsteps.

When we got home, we were all exhausted—Steve from an overseas trip, Jackson and I from walking the hospital floors all night. Everyone was tired and stressed from worry except you-know-who, the other family member, Mr. Rocky Bates, who always had to be the center of attention. We put Jackson in our room for one night to watch him; then Steve fell asleep, and Jackson woke up, crying. Rocky trotted in and stood at the doorway. The star standing in purple Barney pajamas would not be upstaged. With one hand leaning on the doorframe and the other on his pint-sized hip, he said, "I sleep here, too, Mommy."

I yelled, *"I can't take it anymore! I need sleep! I'm losing it!"*

This was the first time that I witnessed Rocky ever give up on an idea he had decided on. He did not like being left out of anything. He stared at his wild mommy, with her hair shooting out and raccoon eyes from mascara, and at his dad, who was glaring at both of us in disbelief. You could see Rocky thinking to himself. He paused for a second and said, "Maybe I go back my bed."

Ready for our usual Rocky battle, we sat there in bed and laughed. He had cased the situation and made the right choice, thank God.

◆ ◆ ◆

Rocky's problems continued. When he tried to run around and entertain Jackson, like dancing on the sofa or jumping on the bed, he would start coughing, which would lead to an asthma attack. Jackson would be laughing and then would see his brother sit down on the floor.

Sometimes if a party's food was loaded with artificial additives or certain fast foods, he would start hitting, biting, or taking kids' toys. (In fact, Jackson owes his agility in sports today to his early training dodging his big brother.) Do you know how many things are bad for a hyper allergic child? He was a child who seemed to be affected by most products that weren't pure. My role consisted of being the neurotic mother running around, knot in my stomach, and grabbing foods away from him, which led to his increased aggravation. It was embarrassing.

Other times Rocky would be invited to a party and would run around with excitement, socializing like he was the host, playing games and swinging at piñatas. It was all about the tipping point. What had he eaten? What was in the environment? Did they have animals or a real dusty house? Did he get any sleep the night before? It was a doubled-edged sword for me; the more I learned, the more stressful it became each day. My love for our family made me read and bone up on health issues, but the more I discovered, the more hectic it became.

Jackson was different. He would go outside, and kids of all ages would gravitate toward him. Teenagers would bring over their skateboards or a soccer ball. I have a photo of Jackson riding on a board in front of our house, his arms out, wearing a big smile. He was less than three.

Jackson was always attracted to balls and airplanes and was content to play for long periods of time alone, unlike his social-butterfly brother, who liked to ride his bike all over and visiting parents, nannies, and kids as if he were running for mayor.

Being sick so often was hard for Rocky. He was always trying hard to win friends, when Jackson had more than he could handle. Always dancing to your own beat is like patting your head and rubbing your stomach. It wears on you and everyone watching. Rocky would try, but I could see it was not an easy task, this thing called play. He was always on a different page in those days.

◆ ◆ ◆

Rocky loved any kind of music, and at a moments notice, he would start dancing as if he were trying out for *Dancing with the Stars*. I remember how one crazy holiday season when I was bringing out the Christmas decorations he spied the Christmas tree skirt. Pulling it on, he twirled his way over to me and beckoned me to dance with him, and then Jackson jumped in on the action. In the grocery store that Christmas, I met a friend who was angsting about her kids. At that moment, Jackson was crawling down the cereal aisle, barking like a dog.

I yelled, "Jackson, stop!" He advised me, "I'm not Jackson. I'm Spot!"

I said to the woman, "Don't tell me your troubles. I have one kid who thinks he's a dog and another at home twirling in a Christmas tree skirt!"

During holidays, the boys would take every chance to sit on Santa's lap and ask for a dog. Well, actually, Rocky would be the only one who sat on Santa's lap. His brother would either scream or stand glued to my leg like a tripod while Rocky made his pitch.

Rocky would ask all sorts of things. "What's it like at the North Pole? Do you have a garage? What do the elves do when they finish making toys?"

Finally Mrs. Claus would whisper to Rocky that Santa had to go and check on his reindeer. Santa probably went for a "double," and I didn't blame him. What kind of person could do that job?

Jackson and Rocky also wrote Santa many times for a dog, but it was out of the question, much as I regretted it. My endless stream of childhood pets had prepared me for many of life's lessons. Having a pet teaches responsibility. Sure, Mom always winds up feeding the animal, but children learn about care and unconditional love. They see that their beloved animals die, and as time passes, they get through it. They learn that someone will always be there for them even if it's a bad day for family and friends.

The animal topic came up often with our boys, but as health issues were our first priority with Rocky, we had to put the dog on a wish and wait list. You could see their little disappointed faces when they ran downstairs Christmas morning and saw yet-another stuffed dog. Rocky finally gave up on the puppy and decided to devote his letters to Santa to asking for a baby sister. Suddenly a dog was sounding better to us. Maybe we could keep the dog outside or wash him more often than usual.

> Dear Santa,
> I wish for God to celebrate his birthday up in heaven.
> And if we can't have a real dog, can we have a baby sister and a Sega Genesis?
> Jackson wants an airplane.
> Rocky

I can't believe it; I was worried about a dumb dog being a health issue for Rocky. Now look at us. What a joke. I couldn't hear his breathing. Wasn't a hospital equipped for breathing problems?

Why were the doctors stopping to discuss the situation again? This was no time to stop and reassess matters. Rocky wasn't moving. A sharp pain in my stomach brought me back into focus.

I should have taken him right from soccer to the hospital, and then he'd be OK. How was I to know this was so serious? We were already in town this afternoon at the school field. Why did I drive home? Would it have made a difference? All these years I always remained calm on the outside for Rocky, and it always turned out. But deep down, I felt a shift, like a small tremor in the earth, a warning of things to come.

Chapter Nine

It seemed that my brother and I were always processing death with our young hearts. Whether it was the demise of the smallest of creatures or a human tragedy, they all, in their own ways, taught us coping methods.

When we grew up, our house was filled with pets that my brother liked to annoy. I still hadn't forgiven him for letting my parakeet Junior, out when we had circus day in our backyard. When I saw the empty cage, I ran screaming to my mom. She suddenly jumped into action. She grabbed a small mirror, ran out to the side of the house for the garden hose, stood in our driveway, and waited for reconnaissance to direct her toward our bird.

"There up in the elm tree; see that bright green spot," a neighbor lady yelled.

"No, where?" My mom shouted like a guerilla fighter.

"Over there. Behind that *V* in the elm branch."

A group of women and children turned their necks upward, shielding their eyes from the morning sun, as if saluting.

"Yes! I see it!" my mother hollered.

She took hold of the hose with her two hands and dragged it across the street. She tried to blast the parakeet down while, at the same time, appealing to his bird vanity with a mirror. There we were, neighbors gathering, all craning our necks to see the little green speck thirty-odd feet high and then slowly turning our gaze toward my mom, who was yelling, "Junior, come to Mama!"

He wasn't coming back, and we couldn't even have a burial service for him.

Soon a new baby parakeet arrived. We named him Pretty Boy. My brother discovered that Pretty Boy was small enough to fit in his Lionel train boxcar. He thought it would be nice to give him a welcoming ride. At first, Pretty Boy wouldn't go in; then the train started up with one bird leg in and one out. After some work, Pretty Boy was loaded in, and the conductor set the train for warp speed. After that, my little bird walked with a limp, and his eyes didn't look right. If you made it in our house, you were ready for anything.

When my childhood pets died, I felt the grief. My mom, brother, and I talked about it. It was a small learning lesson that I didn't understand at the time, but it built a foundation for the future. Dialogue about life and death came early for us; we experienced life's lessons as a family. Going through all the pets and burials in our household and watching animals die at my grandma's farm helped us slowly recognize the circle of life without really being aware of it.

At our makeshift services, we remembered our pets with funny stories, which gave us comfort and helped us to move ahead. Our awareness of the life cycle was a spiritual gift, given to us as children, unbeknownst, by my mother. Her deep devotion to God's infinite wisdom in giving and taking life prepared us for the future. She taught us by example that spirituality was like learning a musical instrument or a sports game. It took practice and work. We wouldn't think of turning up to win a tournament without preparation; neither could we breeze through life without a belief system in place. When a sudden catastrophe or even death showed up at our door, we were as prepared as we could be to see the impermanence of life, or so we thought.

♦ ♦ ♦

One hot summer day my brother and I were in the process of trying to push each other into our pond when my mom called out, "Vicky, get your brother; we're going to Grandma's house."

"Aw, not now, Mom."

"Victoria Ellen!"

We grudgingly trudged up our hill, shoving each other to be the first to plop down in our new turquoise '57 Chevy. Still pushing at each other, we jumped in the back seat and instantaneously skyrocketed out the back, screaming as if we were launched missiles at Cape Canaveral.

My parents always had factory-installed plastic seat covers to keep the car clean for whoever would buy it next. Kids' legs would heal, but car value increased for resale with spotless seats.

Finally we cautiously got into the car and headed to Grandma's farmhouse. As my mother drove down the tree-filled street, she slowed to what seemed a crawl. This made the trip even longer to my brother and me, since we had been pulled away from our mindless fooling around to pick up some fresh vegetables, eggs, and baked goods. We needed to get back before our friends had fun without us; besides, our grandma, who made bread to die for, made cakes you could die from, as she had no interest in specialty dessert items. We had been informed early on that we were on a cake mission. As my mother drove through the streets, the red, blue, and pink bicycles and tricycles parted to the sides. Halfway down the block, we heard a great clanging noise, which was followed by a metal sound under our car. My mom got out and raised both hands to cover her mouth in shock and disbelief. My brother and I jumped out of the back seat to follow my mom and see what we had hit. I heard a man yell from the other side of the street, "Get those kids out of here! A little boy got hit. He's under the car with his bike."

Suddenly two strangers, who had happened to be driving behind us, swooped down, grabbed us by our arms, and turned us away from the scene.

Why were these people pulling us away? We were never to go anywhere with strangers. I was scared; something was happening. Neighbors were gathering. Where was my mom? Did she really hit a boy? I didn't really understand. I heard someone say, "Call an ambulance!"

The man and woman asked about our father. "Where does your daddy work?"

"He has a nursery over there," we said, as we pointed around the corner.

"Let's go for a walk and find him."

We were hustled to my dad's nursery, which was a block away. I wanted to turn around and find my mom, but they wouldn't let us witness the fatal scene. The little boy, about two and a half years old, had darted out from behind some bushes and had been dragged under the car and killed.

That afternoon the phone rang. It was the boy's grandmother, calling to tell my mother that she was a murderer. I saw my mother stand still with the receiver to her ear and then gently place it down. Ghostly pale and shaking, she disappeared into her room. I thought she was sick. I waited for a while and sneaked into her bedroom. She lay there on top of the covers, on her back, her black hair resting across the pillow. I stared at her. It was the same position she lay in for her daily naps, but it wasn't the same Mommy. She didn't seem like she was in there. Why would anyone yell at her? She hadn't done it on purpose. Her normally high blood pressure went even higher, and the local priest was called to comfort her. She was having a breakdown.

Grown-ups have their way of dealing with mishaps. They are given gentle talks, pills by professionals, and drinks by friends. No one was aware that my brother and I needed some medical help in the form of a touch on the cheek and a kind word. We had come into the world with intuition and spirit. But just like learning to talk and walk, we needed someone to show us the way. We didn't know how to honor these gifts ourselves. Toys came with batteries, and children came with parents. I kept my counsel. It seemed to me that our family was penciled in for misfortune every few years. I quickly realized that you could replace your green parakeet with an identical bird and name him the same, and life would go on. But you couldn't do that with people.

As Life Span, at Rhode Island Hospital, puts it,

> One of the most difficult tasks a parent has to face is that of talking about tragedy with their children... When speaking with younger children, remember to emphasize that they are safe and cared for...Be sure to include the facts in a simple way, even if that seems hard for the child to hear. Couch these facts in as warm and supportive a framework as you can; with reassurances that you are going to be there for them...Remind them that questions are okay.

Chapter Ten

Thinking back now, I realize that all those specialists didn't really know what to do with my son. I didn't either, but at least I had my instincts to rely on. The time, money, and nights I spent looking for a way to help Rocky act and feel normal were endless. I went over and over the possibilities. It couldn't be that food alone was causing all these behavioral problems. Nor could everyone's opinions about discipline be wrong. I felt like the salmon heading up stream, against all odds. I would see another professional.

We were sent to the "best" allergy doctor in the area. Going to see all these doctors was a full-time and costly job in itself.

Our appointment was for 9:15 a.m. It was now 10:35 a.m. We had read all the picture books and played with all the germs on the building blocks, and we were now hungry and restless. "The Doctor will see you now." Rocky would not cooperate. A young child did not want to sit still, be probed, and have his chest listened to. What did little kids think? Maybe the stethoscopes listened to secret thoughts in there. He screamed every time the doctor tried to approach him. We had waited a long time. The doctor was short with us.

He turned to me and said, "Mother, step outside. I will handle this. You need to be stronger with this child."

I stepped out, feeling the way I had when Sister Mary Catherine had spoken to me in the third grade. I had been passing around a wallet-size Elvis Presley photo. When she saw my best friend, Patty, peeking at them, we got busted. I didn't even like Elvis;

he had come with my plastic wallet. Sister Mary Catherine was about 110 years old. The hard, white part of her veil rested neatly in a forehead wrinkle above her bushy white eyebrows, like the chrome on an old Buick. I think her tough attitudes were honed from her days of babysitting for Attila the Hun's kids. Now she was Attila the nun.

"I will not have you girls idolizing false gods. Go sit outside Sister Marie's office until further notice. How could you hurt your dear mothers like this?" she proclaimed with a twisted finger directed toward us.

As I sat outside the doctor's office, everyone in the waiting room could hear Rocky crying hard. Maybe the other parents didn't realize it was my child; maybe they thought I was the nanny. I smiled at everyone with that practiced look. Kids, what are you going to do, huh? I wanted to go in but had a habit of doing what professionals told me to do. The longer I sat there, the angrier I became. Wasn't I the mother? I was filled with self-doubt again. Finally the door opened, and I was told to come back in for an evaluation. Rocky glared at me. We both knew I was a traitor. The doctor told us it couldn't possibly be allergies that made my son vomit so violently and continually after eating something. It had to be the flu. No one reacts that severely and for so long because of allergies alone. Once again, it was time for a new doctor.

The naturopath suggested a new "forward-thinking" clinic for children with severe allergies. We underwent the clinic's tests. Rocky sat crying and watching cartoons as he was needled over and over again for a period of two weeks. I was given a book to read. I started by reading the back cover.

The book tutored parents on how to identify the common foods, chemicals, or allergic substances that could be the culprits causing some children to feel unwell, act inappropriately, or be cranky. Rocky certainly fit under the sick and cranky category. They left out headstrong. I met with the head of the clinic.

This elderly doctor, who was slight of height but not weight, sat down beside me. Taking off his old-fashioned glasses, he placed them on his desk and turned to face me.

"It is a shame that many children are abused because they don't listen or seem out of control, when in reality, it is the reaction to foods and environmental elements that make them act out," he said.

Had I finally found the right doctor?

After the tests were completed, we were told that Rocky was so allergic that the antigens could not all fit in one vial and that he needed to have three shots every other day. The clinic was too far from our home, so I was instructed on the art of filling the needle and injecting the shots. Now I was expected to be a nurse? I just wanted to be a mommy, but that was not in the cards. My freezer was filled with medicines. In it, we had at hand all the makings for a painful morning and a good dinner. I was scared to death that I would get air bubbles in the vials and kill my son. I had not one but three chances to do this every other day. I tried to hold him down with my leg while injecting his tiny bottom with the shots.

He was screaming and trying to break free. Did I hit a nerve or something? This crying was harder than the day before. I didn't know how much longer we could take this.

"Rocky, I know it hurts; lie still I don't want to hurt you more. Please, honey, we're almost done. Only one more," I said, knowing that the next day we would go through this again.

I decided at that moment that I was finished with this form of abuse. How many times had he stood still while a nurse put an IV in to take blood in the hospitals? He was such a trooper. I had been giving him shots and taking him for testing for almost a year.

Birds were singing outside in the warm sun, and here we were, flopped across his bed like sumo wrestlers. That sweet face was gazing at me with tears running down it. Rocky's health had not improved enough to justify the pain I was handing out. Enough was enough. I was quitting the shots. I would not be a stressed-out mother torturing her son any longer.

"Rocky, this is the last time for shots. No more, I promise. Let's go to the merry-go-round and have lunch with your buddies. Please stop crying."

I pulled up his Disney underpants and shorts, pulled him to me, and rocked and kissed him over and over again. We would celebrate.

The only lunch friend I could find for Rocky was his sweet friend Annie, who had an idiot for a mother. You know the type. When Annie was a baby, the mom would put super tight headbands on her head so that you would know it was a girl, plus the baby designer glasses with rhinestones. When Annie got home and the headband was pried off, I wondered if her skull was indented the way my plush carpet was when we moved the piano.

I'm sure she talked about me so often dressing my son in black like Johnny Cash.

At lunch, I mentioned to this mom that I wasn't giving Rocky any more shots, and she said, "Well, it just breaks my heart to watch my little Annie get a shot. I have to leave the exam room." Was she kidding? I wanted to smack her in the face and knock her off her chair, not just once but maybe two or three times, just for Rocky. She had no concept of the agony my son endured everyday and the stress it put on me, the provider of that pain.

♦ ♦ ♦

When Rocky started to play with friends, sometimes after a Popsicle or bright candy treat, he would express himself by biting the nearest person.

"Mommy, Kurtie is going for donuts; can I go?"

"Well...you know that isn't good for you."

"Please, Mommy, please; I'll eat it good. Tell Kurtie's mommy."

Carolyn had pulled up outside my house with about four neighbor kids in the car. I bent into the driver's window and looked at all the eager faces.

"Hi, Carolyn, maybe if you could get him a plain one, it would be OK. The chocolate and sprinkles aren't good for him. But it seems like all treats are bad, and he always feels left out."

"We'll all get plain."

"Thanks. OK, Rocky, you can go, but plain, OK?"

"OK, Mommy, I get plain."

A half hour later, he came back crying and pushing his friend around.

"What's that red on your shirt, Rocky?"

"Cherry drink."

"Oh."

The cherry drink that is all artificial flavor and color and the donut? Great, let the fun begin. I couldn't expect everyone to know everything about my son. No one had ever experienced a child this sick. He looked like a healthy boy on the outside, which deceived everyone into thinking he was fine and I was neurotic.

No one, even the few with a vested interest, knew the formula to good health.

I thought that it was just the toppings on donuts that were bad for him and that if I switched to plain, there would be no consequences. Later a nutritionist told me, "Many donuts are fried in old oil. Old oil turns rancid without a smell, which is very bad for food-sensitive people."

One morning trying to earn some Girl Scout points, I attempted to make homemade donuts. My son was not going to be deprived. The dough was like glue. I couldn't get the mixture off the spoon into the fresh oil, no matter how hard I shook the spoon. Of course it came off and plopped on the floor as soon as I turned to answer my son's question. I threw a piece of paper towel over the mess on the floor and started with a new spoonful of dough. The first batch burned. There was certainly no hope for producing donut shapes. The few that weren't burnt came out all deformed and had the look of hash browns with a small dime-size hole toward the bottom. After all the work, I only had four strange looking objects, which I carefully laid out on a paper towel. When I presented Rocky and his two friends with my work, they looked at each other and said, "What are these?"

"These are fresh homemade donuts; don't they look delicious? Try one. They are better when they look like this."

They each cautiously took a bite and put them back on the plate.

"Mommy, can we go to the donut store later?"

Who was I kidding? I had never been a Girl Scout. In high school, I'd put safety pins in my socks when they had holes in the back. When other girls were practicing cheers and helping the nuns, I was in the car with Liz, who was teaching me how to smoke.

After about forty-five minutes of cleanup from my face, shirt, the stove, the floor, various bowls, and utensils—plus the splattered grease everywhere—I sent the kids over to play at a neighbor's house and stretched out on the sofa.

Whenever Rocky and I saw the gardener's truck stop in front of our yard, we stayed in the house or went for a walk. The wonderful aroma of fresh-cut summer grass, which most of us took for granted, caused Rocky's chest to tighten and strain for air, leading to another half-hour treatment.

The treatment consisted of an exact measuring out of his asthma medicine with an eyedropper into a container about the size of a two-inch plastic cup. Next you spray in some measured saline solution that you have shaken. Now you firmly plug the clear plastic tubes into the shoebox-size machine (which when turned on, forces air through the tubes to the medicine cup that in turn forces the medicine and air into the mouthpiece).

By now Rocky's breathing was labored. I pulled a chair over with my foot, plugged the machine into the wall, sat down with Rocky on my lap, and with my free hand placed the flex tube close to his mouth. This was all done in a matter of minutes. He would look at me while coughing and wheezing and ask, "Why...a... do I...a...have...asthma?" As he grew older, he asked the same question. "Why am I the only one who gets sick? I hate asthma; it's not fair." Many times he would start crying.

Once while waiting in a doctor's office, I read an article from the American Lung Association, "Childhood Asthma: An Overview," about asthmatic children and behavior: "Many children with asthma suffer from severe anxiety during an episode as a result of suffocation produced by asthma. The anxiety and panic can then produce rapid breathing or hyperventilation, which further triggers the asthma. During an episode, anxiety and panic should be controlled as much as possible. The parent should remain calm."

Chapter Eleven

It was truly hard to get such a young child to sit still on my lap and inhale mist from a machine that didn't squeak or hop. I resorted to giving Rocky a toy and then trying to hold him on my lap. I would try anything to keep his mind off his body and forced breathing. I had to always remember to have extra medicine on hand. One mistake, and we would have to rush to the hospital.

During a treatment, Rocky would stare out the window at his friends playing on our front lawn. I knew exactly how he felt, as I watched the mothers on the sidewalks chatting and laughing with each other about this and that. At times like this, we both felt so isolated and alone. After about fifteen minutes of treatment, he would start to squirm, and I would have to get even more creative and silly. When the tube sent out only air, we knew the medicine was finished, and I could take him out to continue to play with his little buddies—if they were still around.

We lived in what some considered a picture-postcard neighborhood. Ancient groves of fruit trees, heavily laden with juice oranges, and lush, neatly trimmed greenery framed our Spanish California–style house. In the spring, the overwhelming fragrance that drifted toward our home turned that postcard into a nightmare. One morning within a thirty-minute span, I witnessed a radical change in Rocky. At first, he was playing with a little friend, laughing and sharing toys. Then slowly I saw him turn to anger and crying. Within ten minutes of the behavior change, he was into a full-blown asthma attack and on his way to the hospital.

Some days when there was too much chlorine in the Jacuzzi, I would have to pull him out, away from his buddies, as his breathing tightened to short, small breaths and he searched for air. He would stand in front of me, with that tiny delicate chest, his shoulders pulling up and down for lack of air. Oftentimes he was so used to the tightness in his chest that he would play through it until it would go out of control.

He would cry, "Mommy, I promise [deep breath] I'm okay. Let me stay with [deep breath] my friends, please Mommy. I don't want [deep breath] a treatment. I'll have one later, I promise. I'll just sit on the edge [deep breath] and watch; see, you can sit in your chair and watch me, okay?" He wanted what all little kids wanted—to be the same and not to be singled out because he was different.

I wish I had had the Internet during Rocky's health dilemmas back then. On the website www.kidshealth.org, I came across an eye-opening description of what the victim of asthma goes through during an attack. It was worse than I feared:

> Take a long, deep breath-right now. Inhale slowly, until your lungs can't hold anymore...Now let the air out gradually...ahhh. Breathing feels so natural that it's easy to take for granted, isn't it? Normally, the air you breathe travels effortlessly through your nose and mouth, down the trachea (also called the "windpipe"), through the bronchial tubes into the lungs, and finally to tiny clusters of air sacs, called alveoli. Here, oxygen is exchanged for carbon dioxide in your blood.
>
> Now try something different: run in place for three minutes. Then place a straw in your mouth, close your lips around it, and try to breathe in and

out only through the straw. Not so easy anymore, is it? Now, narrow the straw by pinching it in the middle. Even more difficult to breathe? That's what it feels like when a child tries to breathe during an asthma flare (commonly called an "attack"). During a flare, the airways narrow and become obstructed, making it difficult for air to move through them. Asthma can be very scary—and when not controlled, it can be life-threatening.

Rocky wasn't affected every time he got into the Jacuzzi. Sometimes he would go in for a while and come out feeling fine. I would think that maybe he'd outgrown the allergy. Now looking back, he may have had clean, non- allergic food that day and hadn't been on the brink of that additive tipping point. His allergic body could handle just so much, but there came a point when one added element could push him over if his tiny body was filled to capacity with such things as preservatives, artificial colors, grass, and bad air quality—and the list goes on. The smaller the body, the less it could handle. Oh, how I felt for him.

Standing nearby and watching him while children screamed with delight in the pool behind me, I would be calculating the time it would take us to walk the short block home plus the time it took to fill the nebulizer machine with medicines on the bad days. I had the timing down pat. I couldn't pull him right out every time. Sometimes I gave in for a few seconds, as I was thinking with my heart and not my mind.

I surrendered to those big, brown, pleading eyes. I was acting the uneducated fool by telling myself it was OK once in a while to head to the pool, even while knowing full well that the kids would end up in the hot tub to warm up. I would think that maybe today the kids would stay out of the hot tub or that maybe today the water wouldn't hurt him. I would ask the other mothers quietly, "Do you think you can keep your son or daughter in the pool? The Jacuzzi is hard for Rocky and his asthma."

"Well we'll try, but you know how much Billy and Nicole like that hot tub," they would say smiling, not realizing the severity of Rocky's problems. They thought I was overprotective, and I sometimes wondered if that were true.

I felt he needed emotional bonding with his friends, friends who every day paraded by our house with Dumbo towels and large, brightly colored inner tubes around their waists, who clunked down the sidewalk wearing fins and Big Bird swimsuits, and who said, "Come on, Rocky; we're going to the pool. Come with us."

Once I bought a blow-up two-ring pool, which I placed on our front lawn near the sidewalk. Rocky would sit in it and say to the kids, "Hey, guys, come in my pool. It's so fun; come on."

A few kids came over to splash around, but it held little interest for them, and after ten minutes or so, they would head to the big pool and hot Jacuzzi, leaving Rocky alone and crying. After a while, I would say, "Come on, we'll go for a short while, OK?"

"OK, Mommy. I'll be good."

Did he think he did something bad and was being punished? Was I being weak giving in and not dealing with his health, thinking it was only a little problem? Did I really know how severe his health problems were, that the choices I made could be a matter of life and death?

When he wasn't feeling well, he isolated himself and acted out against the neighbor kids. It was ironic that he was so very social and yet sabotaged himself through unacceptable behavior. When he was feeling good, he was in his zone, very entertaining and funny. He made everyone laugh with his clowning around. Maybe he learned to be extra funny to make up for the not-so-good times. Why did he always have to get an asthma attack when he had the audience right where he wanted them?

I recently learned that "high doses of chlorine in pools and especially hot tubs produce a list of dangerous chemicals." No doctor told me. I don't think they ever connected it because they never had dealings with such a highly allergic child. I knew the chlorine affected him sometimes but thought it was just part of his life, something he'd get over in time. I had no idea of the risk I was taking with my son and his lungs.

According to Allan Finney of Mainstream Water Solutions, "During the Olympic games in Australia more than one quarter of the American swim team suffered from some degree of asthma. Over a short time exposure to such chloramines is like smoking cigarettes to your lungs." So there we were with Rocky's miniature lungs and tiny bronchial tubes trying to suck in air while grown athletes with Olympian health, no asthma, and strong lungs had problems.

Once at an evening picnic, a smoky campfire started an asthma attack and forced us to head home while all of Rocky's friends ran wild, laughing, with sticks and marshmallows. I would watch him, as we had to leave one activity after another, and feel for him each time. As we walked away, his tiny chest was pulling up to get air in.

Another time we attended an indoor rodeo in Los Angeles at the Coliseum. We climbed higher and higher up the bright metal stairs until the horses became the size of our TV screen. Looking down, we could see that the arena below had been transformed from a basketball court to a Western scene with bales of hay, fences, and a dirt-covered floor. Rocky sat between us, not knowing what to expect or why he was there. As we pointed to the cowboys and the wild horses, he started to get excited as he watched us overreact by clapping and yelling ride'em cowboys.

Fifteen minutes into the show, Rocky started to breathe a little heavier, but I thought nothing of it since we were sitting so far away from the animals. A few minutes later his small chest and shoulders were rising and falling rapidly. There we sat, way up high, a good distance from the exit doors and the parked car. You always have that selfish moment when you say to yourself, "Is it really that bad or will it pass?" Quickly his breathing became labored, and when his brown eyes widened with panic, I leaped up. We had brought his small inhaler but didn't realize it was empty. You couldn't visually see the medicine since it was in a metal, three-inch aerosol canister—I had thought we had an extra one in the glove compartment.

Steve, Rocky, and I headed for the nearby hospital in the worst part of LA. We had no choice—it was the closest, and we were in a hurry. Thank God, Jackson had stayed home for a playdate. We were even frightened to get out of the car. When we arrived at the emergency doors, we saw two police officers standing by a scary guy outside the building. Once inside, it seemed like we waited forever, because it was Saturday night and they had gunshot and knife wounds to attend to. The hospital was in full swing. What chance did Mr. and Mrs. Orange County have?

Eventually a nurse appeared and took us to a pale-green, curtained-off back room, and there we sat.

Finally Rocky turned to us and said, "Let's go home. I think I feel better."

The filtered hospital air and time had improved his breathing, and he knew that the treatment the hospital would give was similar to our home care, which came with the added bonus of the *Bambi* movie. After that, we bought a new portable machine, which would plug into the car lighter, for emergency treatments. This small breathing tool could fit inside a case the size a camera case and could fit in my purse or the glove compartment. The filters and container for the asthma meds had to be constantly cleaned and checked before we left the house for any kind of excursion.

A few months later I found myself at McDonald's. I was sitting on a bright, plastic, clown-head seat in the safety of mesh walls and plastic balls. This was the Happy Meal haven, protecting the outside world from screaming, ball-flinging children. Rocky and I had been to another professional about his oppositional behavior. All my well-meaning neighbors had said in one way or another: "Vicky, it can't possibly be food allergies that make your son cry and bite."

I would respond, "You might have a point there," even while I instinctively thought, *I can't believe that's true, but maybe...*

Another version was, "My friend has the name of the top child psychiatrist in Orange County. I'm sure he can help."

Their conversations rolled in and out of my thoughts.

"Can you believe that Chase can drink from a straw already?"
I wish that was all I had to think about.

"Isn't Paula's daughter adorable?"

My Rocky was not only adorable but sharp-witted. If he wanted to, he could stun these mothers with his insight and repartee. My only question was, how could a kid who could make a waitress swoon with one look turn around and sink his teeth into someone?

As I sat in McDonald's, I was going over the morning conversation I'd had with the latest professional. Another waste of time and money.

"If Rockford refuses to listen, put him in a time-out chair."

"And if he won't sit in the chair?"

"If Rockford won't sit in the time-out chair, put him in his room."

"And if he won't sit in his room?"

"If Rockford refuses to sit in his room, lock him in there. He will learn."

This was starting to sound like the children's book, *The Runaway Bunny*. I couldn't sit through this endless rhetoric any longer. The dollars were ticking away. More advice from a "professional" who probably didn't even have children. Our time would have been better-spent chasing ducks around the park.

"Thank you, doctor. I'll give it a try!"

Standing by his gurney, I couldn't help but think of Rocky at the park.

Rocky loved climbing and exploring. He would be the first to try a daredevil stunt on the triple high slide or monkey bars. Mothers would be sitting speechless, mouths open, looking from him to me and back to him, and waiting for me to yell, "Stop! You're too high!"

Neither one of us was fearful. This was the easy stuff, a break in our real daredevil antics, like racing down the Santa Ana Freeway, weaving though traffic, and hoping to reach the hospital in time.

"Mommy, I can't breathe," Rocky would plead, so very frightened.

"We're almost there, just a few minutes. You're doing great, Rocky. The hospital is at the next off-ramp. Hang in there, baby. Mommy is so proud of you."

Chapter Twelve

The appointment with another top psychiatrist had been over an hour ago. As I looked up, the other mothers at the McDonald's were making playdates and rounding up their kids for naps and quiet time. An orange ball came flying toward me from the McDonald's cage. I decided to head home, too. Soon I could try out this new pricey advice.

As I drove home, I thought over what the doctor had said, and somewhere deep inside, I knew it was another form of false hope. I wondered what Rocky thought of this new guy? I let my imagination run wild. Rocky was sitting in the doctor's office with his little legs crossed, as if he were a mini-adult. He was intently filing his nails and nodding his head when the doctor spoke, and then he would look up into the guy's eyes and say, "Yes, I certainly see your point, doctor. I am a little nutcase." He would be thinking to himself, *Another idiot specialist. I could have used this money for that red dump truck at Toys R Us. I can't believe my parents pay for this shit.*

We got home and strolled into the house.

"Rocky, time for a nap."

"I want to play with Kurtie. He doesn't sleep! I want to swim now. I sleep tomorrow, okay?"

The lunchtime additives and whatever else were kicking in.

"Rocky, go for a short nap or no swimming today at all."

"*No! You stupid!*"

I picked him up, marched into his room, and dumped him in his bed.

"If you come out, Mommy will have to lock the door. Do you understand?"

"No!"

As I predicted, we went straight to the head of the class: locked bedroom with child in it.

Rocky screamed, "I want to go swimming *now!*"

He banged his head against the door. They say head banging was for attention; they say to ignore it. Who were "they," anyway? Standing in the hallway, I was yet again truly torn about what to do. Take the top professional advice I had paid for or follow my gut and open that door? How could he bang his head like that? What was going through that little mind of his? Would he still have a little mind left after the banging? If I didn't make a decision soon, I was afraid I would see his head pop through like a moose over a fireplace. What was I to do if doctors didn't have the answer? I opened the door. Had he won, or was I right? My instincts told me to just hold and rock him when these outbursts came up, but people said I would spoil him.

Once again, I felt so alone and confused; my husband was at a loss also—no one seemed to have the answers. The inability to find answers and get help from the medical establishment was so frustrating and maddening. Did people with other chronic illnesses have the same poor results? At least we had a good insurance plan for the constant doctor bills and a paycheck coming in for the naturopath people insurance didn't cover.

When I had an especially bad day and was feeling sorry for myself, I would always think of those parents I would run into late at night during my emergency-room sojourns who were so much worse off than I was. Seeing their courage time and time again made me stronger and more determined to be the mother in shining armor. As Rocky got older, we seemed to get better at knowing his trigger points and avoiding them. If his buddies were going down to the pool, we took a little longer getting there in order to try and avoid the hot tub and shorten his time with the chlorine.

If he were invited to McDonald's, I would ask the mothers to give him Sprite instead of a colored cola drink in order to balance the fried chicken nuggets all his friends ate.

When Steve and I had our first parent conference at preschool, we drove in silence to the appointment. What would she tell us? Was Rocky acting up? Was he biting kids when he didn't get his way? Was he doing his work or disrupting the class? We were afraid of what we would hear. Would they let him stay? Would they give us our deposit back?

Mrs. Peterson greeted us at the door with a big smile and a hardy handshake. She was a tall lady, who towered over the four year olds. She waved her hand over to the tiny table and chairs and invited us to take a seat. She told us that Rocky was bright and gifted, that he was an asset to her class, and that he was ahead in developmental skills, so eager to learn and ask questions.

"Rocky Bates? Our son?"

We looked up at her from those small "seven-dwarf" chairs and fought back tears. Rocky was not easy on any level. Two questions came to mind. Was she just trying to be nice, and why did he pick on us?

Finally we had something to hold on to. We had trouble on our hands, but it was smart.

As we were getting up to leave, she said, "By the way, do you know what Rocky asked me the other day at recess?"

"No, what?" we asked in unison.

"Rocky said, 'Mrs. Peterson, is that an eighteen-hour Cross Your Heart bra you're wearing? I saw it on TV.'"

She was smiling at the door as we left.

A week later Rocky seemed to be getting a cold, and we started to fill him with grape decongestant (loaded with artificial color, flavoring, and alcohol, not an allergy issue at the time), as the doctor had suggested, to keep his lungs as clear as possible, which helped to keep the asthma at bay. He did enjoy the taste. He enjoyed it so much that the next day I got a call from Mrs. Peterson at preschool. He was falling asleep.

"Has Rocky had any special medicine today?"

"No. Why, Mrs. Peterson?"

"Well, he says he is tired and just wants to lie on our little cot."

"I'll be right there."

As I went by his room, I noticed half a bottle of that decongestant gone. Had I not locked it down properly? How much had he had? I had to call the poison hotline, rush to school, and then get him to the hospital. A doctor, who sounded quite young, read me the riot act. Yes, I had screwed up big time.

However, I asked the doctor, "Why do you think they use sleep deprivation in prisoner-of-war camps?"

It was too late to induce vomiting, so while Rocky struggled and screamed in Emergency, the doctor fed a tube down his nose to administer the antidote. Steve and I waited with him, as our friends, Rocky's godparents, Laurel and Frank, rushed in, concerned for his safety. I'm sure they were thinking that maybe this time it was deadly serious. After all, how many times can a child rush to Emergency and come out all right? Laurel and Frank, with all their kids and experience as parents, felt as helpless as we did. Laurel's husband was a take-charge, problem-solver kind of guy like Steve, so it bothered him that no one had answers to help his godchild. No one had ever seen a child go through so much.

"How is he? We just heard the news and came as fast as we could," they said breathlessly.

"He'll be fine," we said, drained from another surprise morning. I repeated the story for their benefit, and once again although I was making jokes to relax everyone, I felt I had screwed up and had come close to losing him.

Three hours later, evaluated and cleaned out with charcoal like a fish tank, Rocky received his discharge papers. Steve, Frank, and Laurel went back to work after making sure we would be all right. Rocky and I went home and ate a hearty lunch of macaroni and cheese as if nothing had happened.

Flipping through Rocky's baby book recently, I saw a list of some of his emergency trips. After the grape-decongestant episode, I can see why there was more than a remote possibility that we were on all computer readouts for "parents to watch," based on the sheer number of emergency room visits—over a dozen.

He was a busy one. Also entered in the baby book was the stitch list: cut his eye learning to walk, stitches. Fell trying to stand on the dishwasher door holding a glass, stitches.

Before you ask why I hadn't been able to catch him, please note that Rocky was fast, aided by asthma medicines, which hype you up like a pot of espresso. Once, he was screaming from an allergy attack (we had just come from playing by a muddy pond, and I hadn't figured out yet that the mold in the pond was a trigger), and he threw himself out of his dad's arms and hit the table with his forehead—blood, stitches.

Another time, he pulled out a large, weighty mortar and pestle (who knew he was so strong?) from a kitchen cabinet. "Don't touch! Don't touch!" Boom! X-rays on his toe to see if it was broken and stitches. Those stitches are taped in his baby book, because when I woke him up from his nap, he handed them to me. Only two years old, and he had the promise of being a competent emergency doctor.

We had so many local Medi-Stop emergency trips that I started to wonder about all the X-rays he was getting. Soon we wouldn't have to turn the lights on for dinner.

The constant buzz of friends echoed down the hospital hall over into the emergency room.

"You know, if they were in Salt Lake City, they would have better machines to keep Rocky's heart going."

"Too bad Salt Lake is five hours away."

"Well, that's what worries me about living in a small town with this old hospital. We are so limited on the state-of-the-art equipment. It's too bad."

"Did they get a hold of Steve yet?"

"No," said some unfamiliar voice.

"Vicky, is there anyone else we should call for you?" said the hospice woman standing next to me. I couldn't think.

"They are inserting another tube into Rocky; let's hope this helps," she said as she touched my hand.

"Rocky, Mommy loves you. You'll be all right; you always come through, baby."

Chapter Thirteen

In 1994, we decided to move to an environment that would be less stressful for all of us. California had become too overpopulated and too nerve-racking. We moved to Idaho or, as our friends would call it, "Idahoareyounuts?"

Idaho offered us fresh clean air, a multitude of outdoor sports, and great schools. In the past, Steve had had business in Idaho, so we had visited Sun Valley and the surrounding areas a few times. There was a small airport in Sun Valley that connected Steve to Salt Lake City and then on to anywhere in the world for business. It wasn't the easiest routing system, but it was worth it. Upon arriving, people who had come before welcomed us. They, too, had had fears of this new, tranquil life and leaving the fast lane behind. Everyone introduced everyone else. It was like a giant Tupperware party, only it got cold, really cold.

Living in a ski town was completely different than California or where I grew up in the Midwest. It seems funny now, but the hardest thing for me to get used to was the lack of a large city newspaper on my driveway in the morning and numerous radio stations. Riding in LA, I could punch buttons at whim; there were rock, jazz, Republicans, Democrats, gay rights, bible studies, psychiatrists, cooking segments, and so much more.

Now it was country and seventies tunes. There was something about the country music and riding along the open land, though. Listening to songs like "I'm Basting My Turkey with Tears" and "I Got You on My Conscience but at Least You're Off My Back" made you thirst for a longneck beer and a rodeo. It was comforting. The crème de la crème of rodeos was in the small town of Mackey, about an hour east of us. I knew it was the real thing, because I was the only one wearing red lipstick with my new cowgirl hat.

There was no road rage. Traffic jams only happened when herds of sheep came down from the north for the winter. The local papers came out on Wednesday. If an accident happened on Tuesday, you wouldn't see it in print until the following week. If someone was having a problem, the whole town knew and had an opinion before the person became aware. Then there was the fun of everyone running into a spouse with his or her new significant other after a breakup. Once in a while, you could see a couple of local people in the background, heads leaning toward the middle of a restaurant table, vying to get the inside scoop. This happens in large towns, too, but everything is magnified in a resort area.

On the other side of the coin, if someone became seriously ill or lost a loved one, the town would rally together immediately and help with meals for weeks on end, fundraisers, and schooling for children. There was no end to their generosity. This was the spirit of a small town.

In order to let people know he was still accessible in Idaho, Steve was traveling a lot in the first year. No one was aware of what we had been through over the years, and in the beginning, I was desperate to talk with someone who knew our history. That first year was hard. Even in the best of circumstances, they say it takes two years to feel comfortable in a new area.

We were in a rental house with the owner's leftover furniture: a truly frightening, orange, shag carpet, bright-yellow, plastic counter stools, and leaking windows. I would lie on the broken-down bed, which sank like a hammock, and think, "What have we done?"

We moved to Idaho in what they call "slack" season, when no one was in town. It was dead. If able to, locals left; it was not ski season but not yet spring. Many restaurants and shops closed. School was on break. It was rainy, with dirty leftover snow, and I felt trapped in the middle of a state, many miles from a city. We had left all our friends. I had two kids and hadn't figured out what to do with them yet.

All our belongings were in storage until we bought a house. Women need their nesting materials. So I was hit with a double whammy; I was in an unfamiliar house in an unfamiliar town often by myself while Steve traveled for business. Then with summer on the horizon, the people came back like the swallows to Capistrano. There were kids' camps, wildflowers, friends, and a feeling of belonging. We started to shop for a house. The Sun Valley/Ketchum area was not like the rest of Idaho. Every house I liked was close to, or over, a million dollars. The ones on the market in our price range looked worse than the tract homes in California with no land. It was discouraging.

So much for our friends saying, "Boy, you guys are going to really get an unbelievable house when you move. They must be in the one hundred thousand dollar price range or lower in 'Idahoareyounuts?'"

After what seemed like an endless tour of homes with our patient realtor, we found a house on an acre of land resting on the confluence of two rivers and overlooking a mountain with eagles and elk. It was a strange, tall house, like a sleeping giant and needed a family to love it and a special decorator's eye. The house was grandfathered in, which meant no other houses could be built over the river due to environmental restrictions. We had stumbled upon a piece of heaven. The living-room windows were fifteen feet high and hung over the water below. People fished for trout along the banks. Many years ago American Indians had lived in this area, and you could still feel their spirituality.

Just after we moved in, Rocky started first grade. He entered a private school that was highly rated for academics. At the Community School, he excelled in math, reading, sports, and acting. However, in the beginning, he had a hard time fitting in and only wanted to go back to California. The kids in his class knew each other from the previous year, and he felt like an outsider. We should have known that this would happen. Many times he cried and felt like an outsider even with his old friends in California. It was either "My skin's darker than everyone else's" or he was too sensitive and a casual remark on the playground would easily hurt his feelings. He hadn't yet realized how handsome and funny he had become. That realization would come with the change of seasons and a few friends.

He said to Steve, "Dad, how come I have everyone over to my house and no one invites me?" and "Nobody likes me. I want to go back home to California."

Teachers and sympathetic parents helped us. We needed to be supportive but not baby him. I sought professional advice about this new dilemma. *How exciting,* I thought, *a whole new state to go through for professional advice.*

"Rocky is having trouble reading a room," said the counselor. "He needs to be at school early so that when children come in, he can greet them. He doesn't feel comfortable pushing himself into an established group." That advice helped. Now it was only every other day that I would pick him up at school and find that he had been crying on the playground. He was too needy for friendships to fit in.

Then Rocky met a girl named Juliet, who marched to her own drum. At the time, she was a tomboy, an outsider in the class because she didn't enjoy girly-girl things. She was bigger and stronger than Rock. He loved meat and tried to avoid fruits and vegetables; she was a vegetarian who ate everything natural and never ate junk food. Blessed with a new confidante, each gave the other a foundation to pursue additional friendships, and that changed the playing field. The love of a friend brings a feeling of worth, and there is strength in numbers on the playground. Rocky started to feel good about himself and ever so slowly with the other kids.

Jackson, on the other hand, never had a problem attracting friends. They all wanted to come over, or else they invited him to their houses. Rocky couldn't figure out why Jackson was such a draw, which only made him try harder and become jealous of his brother. Yet Rocky never had a problem conversing with adults. Everyone from our hairdresser to his friends' parents was enchanted with his talk and genuine compliments. He was born with that magnetism and sharp wit, but unlike children who had trouble conversing with adults, Rocky had trouble interacting with his peers. Finally something clicked. Rocky's humor and friend-ships started to grow. He helped his classmates with math and could always be counted on to stand up for children if they were being bullied on the playground.

On the first day of fourth grade, he walked into his previous year's classroom and said, "Hey, what are you guys doing here?"

As the kids laughed, they yelled, "Rocky, you are across the hall, in fifth grade now."

"Oh, I've moved up," he said with a grin.

Meanwhile, Jackson was having his first preschool experi-ences. Every time I dropped him off, he would start screaming. He was always content, so I never expected him to wig out at school. I thought he would find it fun with his brother gone during the day. But strange, towering teachers and an unfamiliar envi-ronment sans brother brought out a new side of him. I was use to Jackson being the easy one, but now I had a new development on the horizon.

"Go ahead and go, Vicky; he'll quiet down as soon as you leave."

One hour later, I would get a call.

"We tried every possible idea. We've used all the tricks in the book, and he's still crying quite hard. Maybe you better come over."

I would trudge into the preschool, and there he would be, crying, arms reaching up toward me. I would pick him up and try to calm him. Why was I in such a hurry for my kids to grow up? He was one of the youngest in the class. There were times I had to drop what I was doing with my design business (I had gone back to work on a part time basis, mostly to meet people) and rescue him. I admonish myself now if I ever expressed to him the feeling of inconvenience.

I couldn't always be the perfect mom with perfect kids—sometimes life just happened. One of the boys would get sick or have a fight at school, or when they were really tired and mad, they would say they wanted their "real" mother. It didn't faze me in the least; I couldn't be sensitive about things like that. When I was young, there were many times that I had thought I was adopted and that someday my real parents would come for me.

I would talk with the back of my head, as mothers did while driving, and say, "I might not have given birth to you, but I am your mother. And I will gladly help you find your birth mother when you're eighteen. But for now, put that seat belt on and zip it."

On certain days, I would have my own dialogue going on internally. *Yeah, good idea, let's pull over. Call your mom and have her pick you up this afternoon, you little jerk.*

An hour later one or both would be sitting on my lap, kissing me, and smiling. I would always answer any questions they asked about their birth parents. This question came up a few times through the years: why did she give me away? I couldn't say, "They loved you so much, they gave you up," because that would lead to "Will you give me up?"

How could someone give away someone he or she loved? I tried to explain in simple terms, as soon as they could understand, the fact that they were adopted and the reasons why a mother would give her child up.

"Did my mother have long hair?" Rocky would ask.

"Yes, Rocky. She had very long, pretty hair."

That really threw me for a loop, because his birth mother had hair down to her waist—how strange he asked that question. After repeating the story of how I saw the boys for the first time in the hospital, how we selected each other, and how blessed I felt to have them in my life, they would interrupt me to say, "Okay, thanks, Mom. Nickelodeon is on."

Raising children was a juggling act. I was always trying to keep the balls in the air, and sometimes one would drop. It had been a long road so far for us. We were adjusting to a totally different environment and new friends. Rocky seemed to be improving health wise, and Jackson, in his own quiet way, was getting accustomed to school. Our friendships were limited in the beginning, so we spend more quality days together as a family, which was good. Many times sitting on our deck with the kids, our conversations would be interrupted by a low-flying eagle overhead or a huge beaver swimming by our house. The first time, we thought the beaver was a fat chocolate Lab (city folk). Another time during the spring run off, a sheep went down our river at full speed, baaing for anyone from its group. Spring was the time of year when they were trailed to the north for summer grazing.

As a mother, I had finally learned not to protect my sons all the time and to relax. My job was to just be there, to know when to pick them up and when to leave them where they fell. I also learned a very important lesson from listening to other seasoned parents at school. I had kept a lot of my problems to myself when we had moved to Sun Valley, but I started to notice other mothers talking freely about their sons still peeing in the bed or biting the dog. That information was so freeing to me. Every parent had issues; there weren't any perfect children or parents out there.

We all adjusted to living in Idaho. I found out that national newspapers could be delivered to my front door, and I discovered the National Public Radio station hiding in my radio.

We were within driving distance of such incredible sights as Yellowstone Park and Old Faithful. With no preplanning, we could literally pull off gravel roads to hike, camp, or fish. We had picnics along the Snake River. We snowmobiled in the Sawtooth Mountains and had skiing five minutes from our door. It was an outdoor fairyland for all. There was a point, though, when I started to wonder if I were the adopted one in the family. I loved nature, but sports were not my preferred pastime. The boys and their dad were different. In the beginning, my favorite nature experience was going on scenic drives to historic landmarks like Target, an hour and one-half south. It was a pleasant trip through the mountains and sagebrush, where I could spot hawks, deer, and antique shop signs.

Finally the timing seemed right. Christmas was coming, and we decided to surprise the kids with a special delivery from Santa, a chocolate Lab puppy. Yes, it was a Hallmark-card moment. We had asked around and scanned the papers for a Labrador puppy, but it was winter. It was impossible to believe we couldn't find a dog, seeing that the ratio of Labs to people in Sun Valley was about two to one.

My friend said, "There will be a bigger selection in the spring. It's like forcing tulip bulbs—the wrong season for animals. Try to wait."

The boys had waited long enough. Rocky seemed to be doing better. We would keep the dog out of the sleeping areas and see what happened.

We found a breeder in Buhl, about an hour and forty-five minutes south of us. Steve and I went down to see the puppies. There were only two females left.

We picked one out and asked, "If we leave her here for a few weeks until Christmas, how will we know which one is ours when we come back?"

"Oh, why don't you take that little puppy down to King's discount store and get her a collar? Then we'll know," the breeder said. "You just head on out to the right and make another right on Main Street; then you'll see the thrift store, and right past that park, there's King's."

Leaving no ID or money, we took off with the puppy in my arms and shopped for a collar. The breeder would have been out of puppies in a second if she'd operated like this in New York. A simple agreement still meant something in a small town. We returned with the puppy, which was now wearing an orange collar the size of a Mason-jar lid.

When the boys came downstairs Christmas morning, peeking out of a blanket-covered basket was a wet nose and two brown, button eyes. The boys froze and just stared for a minute. We wondered why they didn't just run over to the plastic laundry basket. They couldn't believe it was a real dog. They were in shock. Rocky decided to name her Sizzle, and from that day, they were inseparable. She was his confidante when things weren't going well and a pillow when he was watching television. She was even used as a scary anaconda, after the movie *Anaconda* came out, to chase the boys around the yard.

"Does Sizzle like playing an anaconda?" I would ask.

Jackson would say, "Oh, yeah, she really runs fast and even grabs us around the legs. It's hard to get her off."

In the winter, she went sledding and played catch with snowballs. Jackson loved Sizzle and used her like a headrest, too, but the love between Rocky and his dog was a bond that could not be broken. She was the recipient of a thousand kisses, against my wishes, and the topic of many a school paper. Once in a while, his asthma would flare up, and I had to think it was partially the dog's fault. But emotionally, Sizzle was extremely important to Rock.

The dog was not allowed on the beds, and I tried to keep her out of the bedroom. But boys will be boys, and once in a while, when I would go in to say goodnight for the last time, I would spy a brown tail ticktocking out of the comforter.

"Rocky, what did I tell you about the dog? Dog hair is very bad for you. Where you sleep needs to stay totally clean."

"What? OK, I'll get her off. She was so cold on the floor; she was shivering."

"Yeah, right."

Everyone in town knew Jackson, Rocky, and his dog, Sizzle, the brown chocolate Lab with the funny name.

◆ ◆ ◆

A few months later we were standing at the Hailey airport when we saw the small prop commuter slowly bounce down and ease onto the tarmac. Grandma and Grandpa had touched down for a visit. The whole building was the size of a Pizza Hut restaurant and was situated between two mountains. We waited at gate one; they arrived at gate two. It was not a confusing airport. On many days, the planes could only land in Twin Falls, about an hour and one-half bus ride south, because of winds, snow, fog, or rain.

Every time I came gliding down through the valley surrounded by green mountains and the Big Wood River, I felt a true sense of being home, and even though I was not a huge cold-weather fan, there was a spiritual and creative quality about the valley. Maybe that's why Hemmingway loved it.

My parents seemed worn as they plodded toward us. Their early morning flight started in Chicago and required a wait and change of planes in Salt Lake City.

Everybody kissed each other and headed for the baggage claim.

Now that the years had passed and my brother and I were gone, my dad had quit drinking, and things were different at home for my mom.

My mom could tell my dad to go out for lunch with my brother, who lived nearby, and she could go on an outing. Unlike the old days, when she'd always had to be home before twelve to prepare lunch, she now, after forty years of marriage, had a sense of freedom from all that stress.

As we were standing around making small talk, my mom looked me up and down. "Where did you get that dress, honey? I love it."

"Target, Mom; isn't it great?"

"Is this the same daughter who only shopped at places like Neiman Marcus?"

Steve waited for their luggage and caught up with my dad. The kids practiced sliding on the baggage drop, and I went to get the car in the parking lot. As I circled the lot, I thought about how I saw my parents in a different light now that Steve and I had two children.

Rocky and my dad had a special bond because of their mutual chronic illness—asthma. My dad, who had suffered his whole life gasping for air, related and connected with his grandson.

When my dad would come back from a Mexican vacation, he would bring some asthma inhalers that he'd got at a good price for Rocky.

"I know how the poor kid feels; it's not any fun, is it?" my dad would say as he patted Rocky on the back. Many times I would catch my son staring at my father and trying to figure him out. Who was this old guy? My dad, who could never be confused with Mr. Rogers, would toughly put his arm around Rocky, shake him, and say, "How ya doin, guy? Brought you some asthma medicine."

I'm sure that excited my son. Rocky probably was thinking, *Asthma medicine, who needs that? We have that at home. Why couldn't he bring a Nintendo game?* But Rocky worked so hard to be loved by my father and get his approval. I knew how he felt and mentally wished him luck.

My dad was nice to my boys whenever he saw them. But he wasn't much on chitchat, and the distance between Illinois and Idaho was not conducive to frequent visits. It really amazed me how he held his tongue when Rocky or Jackson would act out or grow impatient in a restaurant.

Had my dad learned to be calmer, or was he just worn out? Other times when we would visit him, I could see he was on the verge of raising his voice but then would think better of it. It must have been hard after so many years of undivided attention from his daughter to try and have a conversation that was constantly distracted by her two kids. If the six o'clock news was on, that was sacred silent time. The weather report was sacred silent time, but the most sacred silent time was during the commercials, which my father watched over and over again. We could never speak, because everything was earth shattering and important. When the news was over, the kids would come around for a back rub or a jump on his lap for a story.

Driving home, my dad talked about the old days when he used to hitchhike through Idaho and catch fresh trout for breakfast on the Salmon River. He told the boys about watching the Hoover Dam being built and riding the rails during the Depression. The boys were interested in Grandpa's stories about traveling and catching fish, but they didn't think eating them in the morning would taste as good as waffles with tons of syrup. They made a plan to go to a stocked trout pond the next day and try their luck.

While the boys were busy pumping Grandpa with questions and making him laugh, I turned to my mom to catch up on what was going on back home in Wheaton.

"What's happening at home, Mom? Anything new?"

"Well, honey, I have something to tell you. Remember that canary you gave me last year?"

"Yeah."

"He's OK, but...I was vacuuming his cage Monday when he got sucked up into the hose. I called your brother, who was working next door, and he ran over. Of course I shut the vacuum off and shook the hose, but the bird had totally vanished. Your brother took the vacuum apart, and there was little Duke sitting in the bag covered in soot and carpet fuzz with his two beady eyes looking at me. We rushed him to the sink and washed him off, and, knock on wood, he seems fine."

"Oh my God, I bet he cowers in the corner of the cage when he hears the vacuum!"

"I don't clean his cage like that anymore."

It was comforting to know that some things never changed in our house.

Chapter Fourteen

There was a reason the Sun Valley camping book had warned that at a certain point, the road narrowed and deteriorated, which required extra caution and a high-clearance vehicle. Glancing out the car window, I saw rocks tumbling down the side of the mountain below; hanging on to the door handle at this point was like hanging on to a drink umbrella when the captain told you the plane was rapidly losing attitude. I could see the local paper: "Family of four plummet three hundred feet down mountain into rushing river; film at eleven."

"*Steve!*"

"Do *you* want to drive?"

Ah...yes, I said to myself.

We were headed for another trip, just like Clark and Ellen Griswold in *National Lampoon's Vacation*. Sizzle was leaping back and forth over the boys and drooling all over our dinner while the boys laughed and encouraged her with potato chips. I tried to relax and wondered if I had brought any aspirin. Rocky and Jackson thought that this camping expedition was great fun, like an amusement-park ride, swerving high up in the Pioneer Mountains. Soon I saw the open parking area ahead and calmed down.

We pulled into the grassy space and took a sigh of relief. The boys were already out of the car and peeing into the river while the dog stood knee-deep near them and drank the same water. What the fascination was about peeing in the great outdoors, I'd never know.

Next was the tent. Steve and I could never figure out how to get the tent up. To us, putting up this temporary home was as much fun as putting up Christmas tree lights. As if they were professional campers who could not stand watching two inept people any longer, the boys would say, "We'll put the tent up. You guys can go and sit down." Steve would pull out the folding chairs, open a bottle of wine, grab the remaining potato chips, and sit back, and within minutes, it was ready. Wow, weren't these kids the cutest.

We camped out numerous times because it required no planning. In the evening, the boys would fight for the middle spot in the tent in case of bears. We woke our kids up in the middle of those summer nights to come out and see the stars. There were lots of stars due to our altitude and the lack of light for miles around.

We would pull by the side of a road and make a pilgrimage to see a dead animal and try to figure out what caused its demise. We turned up stones and got ready to run from hiding snakes.

We made snow houses and ate lunch in them.

We traveled a lot with the kids, and because of Steve's work, we sat in first class by using frequent flyer miles. Oh, how they loved first class. Jackson's legs were so short that they stuck straight out when sitting next to Rocky. Other adults would walk by our two boys and give them an amused look. The hours Steve spent on the road away from his family, sitting in airports, missing flights, and dinners at home, were a sacrifice so that we could appreciate the perks of riding up front together; besides, it is hard to turn right and head to the back of the plane after you've tasted the perks to the left. When we flew coach, Jackson or Rocky would say, "Where is the lady with the soda?" They were used to sitting down and immediately getting service with a smile before takeoff.

"Aren't you two boys cute, and with such good manners. What would you like to drink before takeoff?" the stewardess would say with a twinkle.

Now in coach, I had to break it to them.

"You see that cart, way in the back? You have to wait for that to move up, like the rest of the people. That is the real world back there; up there is special."

"Oh," they both said quietly.

Jackson leaned his head out over Rocky to find the soda cart but instead witnessed a very large woman pushing and squeezing through the rows, coming toward us. "Wow, she must have a big bachina," he said in a loud voice.

"Jackson, what did you say?"

Rocky couldn't stop laughing.

"Rocky, did he hear a similar word from you?"

"No, Mom."

"Jackson, we don't say things like that."

"Like what?"

He obviously didn't know what he'd said, but as he loved the fact that his brother thought he was funny, it was repeated for more laughs.

"I only said she had a big china."

Jackson always depended on Rocky to be the front man and pave the way, especially when traveling. He would look to his brother even before answering a question.

"Where are you boys from?"

"My brother and I live in Idaho," Rocky said. "We used to live in California, but our parents made us move. I still miss my friends, but I have nice friends now at my new school."

"Where is that?" the stranger asked.

"Sun Valley, Idaho, in the mountains. We used to live ten minutes from Disneyland. I've been on the Matterhorn about twenty times. My brother can't go; he's too small, and that really makes him mad."

"Rocky, let the man read his paper."

Rocky turned to the stewardess and said, "Bet you are surprised I speak English, with my dark skin."

I almost spit my Pepsi across the aisle. He wasn't that dark, but we lived in Idaho, not downtown LA.

We were on our way to Mexico for spring break. Everyone was excited about heading for the warm weather. We often met our neighbors, the Masons, on these trips; they had two kids, Olivia and Hank. The men could golf, and the kids could entertain each other while the mothers read and relaxed. As parents, we realized that traveling alone as a family was not the close-knit bonding experience we had read about. That touchy-feely idea had left us while we'd waited in the Delta airport lounge before takeoff the first time.

"He ate all his candy, and now he wants mine."

"Stop pushing me."

"I'm going to tell Dad what you said."

"Your bag had more candies."

"Don't sit so close to me."

"You're not the boss of me!"

"Mom, do I have to give him the window seat? He always gets the window seat."

"Do not."

"Do, too."

"You don't even like airplanes," Jackson said.

"Yes, I do."

"No!"

"Yes, I do."

What happened to the kids who called each other "buddy" and "pal" at home? The little darlings were forgetting their manners, and we were sitting in the quiet Crown Room for Delta.

Then Jackson said, "I think I'm going to throw up."

"Hurry; let's get to the bathroom," I said, while looking around for a trash can.

Jackson started to heave, and all I could do was cup my hands in front of his mouth.

"Ooh, he threw up," Rocky yelled.

"I'm sorry, Mommy," Jackson said.

"Don't worry; it's OK. Stay with your dad and brother. I'll be right back. I'll get you a damp cloth and some saltine crackers."

All the suits were staring as I ran through the carpeted lounge and tried not to spill.

Then Rocky, all lovey-dovey, piped in with his big-brother routine, leaned over, and wrapped his arm around Jackson.

"I'll take care of you, little buddy. You can have the window seat. OK?" Rocky said, patting his brother gently on the back while looking him in the face like he was a new puppy.

"OK, Rocky. Thank you," whispered Jackson.

Still bending over, Rocky said, "Do you want some of my candy?"

"No, thanks, Rocky," said Jackson quietly.

♦ ♦ ♦

Upon arrival, while working our way down to the Mexican beach-front, Rocky stopped dead in his tracks and looked at a sleeping, topless woman with about a 42 DD bra size.

"Mom, why isn't she wearing clothes on top?" he whispered. Here we go again.

"Well, Rocky, some people enjoy the sun, the body is beautiful, and many countries have different customs."

"But, Mom, they're like big watermelons."

"And what's wrong with fruit?"

"Funny, Mom, very funny," he said with a grin, his innocence eroding away before my eyes.

At the beach, the boys rode the waves with their dad and never tired of making big Jacuzzi holes near the breaking tide. There they would dig and dig until they had the right dimensions for a proper tub. From time to time, they would stop their work and sit down, measuring its depth. Soon Jackson would start to disappear into the hole; about that time, he would get bored and be ready to relax. Rocky, the foreman, would order him to dig another few inches or run for a bucket of water. Off he would go, his shorts almost touching the sand, dragging the plastic bucket Rocky had handed him. He would sit at the breaking water, his butt nearly touching the beach, balanced on his two small feet, waiting for a wave. After scooping up half a bucket of sandy water, he ran back, spilling most, and passed it over to the waiting foreman.

"Is this all you got? Where's the rest of the water? This won't do anything."

"That's all there is, Rocky."

"I guess I have to do everything myself."

Jackson would happily jump back into the hole.

When finished, they would sit, look out at the ocean, and wait for the rushing tide to rise up and fill their spa. Passing kids and adults asked questions; some little kids even joined them in a soak. They would only come out for refreshments. Wiping their sandy faces and hands off on my clean towel, they would grab for chips, hot dogs, and virgin piña coladas. This was living.

I remember one night, sitting in an open-air café touted as fine Mexican dining. We were ready for this after days of tacos and rice.

When dinner came, my friend turned to her little daughter and said, "No elbows on the table, sweetheart."

I looked at my two and said, "Boys, no elbows on the table," with a motherly smile.

Rocky eyed me with amusement. "Mom, you never tell us that at home."

Jackson picked up his lead. "Yeah, Mom, you never tell us that at home."

I laughed, tilting my head like some 1940s movie star. "Oh, kids, you know that's not true."

I thought to myself, *I'm going to kill them when we get back to our room.* Rocky's asthma was improving, but this kind of repartee about our manners could easily be his demise. We wanted them to have a sense of whimsy, but please.

By the time we headed back through customs, Rocky and Jackson were quite tan. With pockets loaded down with shells and rocks, the customs official suddenly stopped them. The man stared at Rocky and asked him his father's name; Rocky paused, looked at Steve, and then, with a quizzical expression on his face, looked back to the official. "Steve?"

At the time, I thought Rocky was being funny because of his dark tan and Steve's pale skin, but maybe he was confused.

♦ ♦ ♦

I felt that the move to Idaho, the new schools, and new friends had put Rocky in control and given him symmetry and balance. He was radiant. Jackson, who was introduced around by his big brother, had no clue about his brother's health history. The difference was that Jackson had arrived on a beam. Everyone wanted to hold and touch him. He was the Buddha boy, calm and peaceful. He looked at the world and his brother with wonder; he was harmony, the missing ingredient to our family recipe.

The second year in Idaho, Rocky was about eight and started to relax and make friends. He met many of his classmates on the ski slopes but had to carry an atomizer because of the altitude. After time, his body seemed to get use to the thin air. He didn't enjoy taking his medicine out and drawing attention to himself by stopping on the slopes as his buddies flew by.

Both boys and girls were calling the house to make playdates. It took him a while to get comfortable. But his teachers and classmates made him feel special, and he started to repay them with grace and compassion. Thanks to his own experiences of feeling left out, he learned to be kind and sensitive to others. He was not a saint, but he was a happy boy, on his way to some sense of fulfillment.

That was the year he started wearing a bright-fuchsia baseball cap with a long fake ponytail attached. It was a gag gift from his godfather, Frank, but it gave him an idea.

In second grade, he decided to let his hair grow long. He had such a beautiful face that it made him look feminine. Many kids made fun of him at first, but he had made up his mind. When it started to get to his shoulders, my husband couldn't take it. "Why does he always have to push the envelope and be so different? It alienates him from his peers; doesn't he see that? We have to insist on him cutting it, no matter what he says. We are the parents. Kids are making fun. I just want to help him to fit in better."

For years, Rocky had embarrassed us by his public outbursts; now he found a new irritant, hair.

My gut told me it would break his spirit, and I was now listening to that inner voice more and more.

On a school outing, I heard his friends not tease but ask him, "Rocky, why did you grow your hair? How long are you going to grow it? Will you ever cut it?"

"Maybe someday; I don't know," he answered.

When we went on vacation, someone said, "What a pretty daughter you have."

Jackson glanced at me, and we both turned to see if Steve had heard the remark.

Rocky said to me, "I guess you're going to have to expect that if you have hair like mine."

Steve made a lot of sense, but I was determined to hold my ground, even if I had a few doubts floating around. Rocky's grades were fabulous. He was involved in sports, and he didn't take the legs off of insects. So what did it hurt to ride this out for a while even though it was hard?

Finally one day in McDonald's, Rocky was coming out of the men's restroom when a man said, "Hey, honey, you went in the wrong room."

Why this time made a difference, I don't know.

That night while I was putting Rocky and Jackson to bed, Rocky said, "I think I'll cut my hair tomorrow and surprise the kids."

I smiled. He could have got anything by the way of a bribe from Steve to cut that hair.

I got into bed that night and said, "Oh, by the way, Rocky wants to cut his hair tomorrow."

"You're kidding," said Steve.

A day later he shocked everyone at school when he appeared with short hair and said nothing. He was enjoying this moment of attention and all the looks from the girls. Something changed inside of him that day. He had controlled his own destiny. He didn't have control over his asthma, but he could be his own person on other issues.

He always liked to say, "It's my body," but no one would listen. For years, they took blood, gave shots, and probed him with tests, X-rays, and needles. At times, he felt like an experiment. Now he was taking charge in a big way.

The following week at breakfast I asked Rocky what time it was. The school bus did not wait around. Suddenly he plopped his leg up on the table, looked at his ankle, and said, "Ten to eight." He was wearing his watch around his ankle.

There I sat at the table, coffee cup paused in midair and my mouth agape. It wasn't so bad.

At home, Rocky was trying all new sports for his dad. Some he liked; some he didn't.

Soccer was a joy to him because of his natural speed, and he loved fencing because of the movement and grace of that individual sport.

His dad's love of baseball didn't transfer to Rocky, though Rocky gave it his best effort. In the summer, he had asked his dad if he would help him learn baseball. Of course that delighted Steve, since he had played baseball in college. Rocky had no prior experience but made the team with help from his dad. His first game was a disaster. He had no friends on the team, as he had in soccer, and he felt and looked isolated from everyone when he needed to use his asthma atomizer, which furthered his embarrassment. After being hit with a hard ball during practice, he was intimidated at the plate and was not feeling well from his asthma. He ended the game on the bench.

No matter how you tried to stay ahead of the asthma attacks, you never knew when they would jump out and surprise you. It could be a week, or it could be days or even hours. Was it the dust at the field? Was it the running? Had he eaten something with a lot of additives that, with the dust and running, had compounded his heavy, labored breathing? Or was it fear of playing and trying so hard that caused his shortness of breath?

On the long walk to the car, Steve wrapped his arm around Rocky and asked how he was doing. Rocky said he didn't want to play baseball again.

"I only did it to please you, but I hate it," Rocky said.

Steve was touched; he reassured Rocky that he was proud of him for trying so hard.

♦ ♦ ♦

In 1997, on a cold Idaho evening, I received a phone call. My father had died. He had been sick off and on for a while, but finally his heart gave out. I wanted Steve and the boys to go back with me for the funeral. Friends said the boys, who were then eight and five, were too young, but I didn't agree. Death comes so much harder to people who have been steered away from it.

Humans aren't wired to learn by on-the-job training when it comes to sudden emotional pain. We need some sense of God and of a higher order. We must enlighten ourselves to the fact that spirituality is a tool that nudges and prods us along when our human minds are frozen into shock. It helps us to acknowledge that hurt is a part of everyone's life journey so that we can face it and move through it. The alternative is to stand still and face the bottomless well of hopelessness.

My father's death offered the boys an important introduction to the cycle of life and death. When Steve brought them into the funeral room, I tried to prepare myself. I thought about what I would say when they saw the stillness of their grandfather before them. They came up close to stare.

Rocky was in third grade, Jackson in kindergarten. They asked if they could touch Grandpa. They touched his hands. I told them that Grandpa was not here but was an angel watching over them, that he had been sick for a long time, and that he loved them very much. I explained that what they were seeing now was just like the seashells that we found at the beach, that the spirit of Grandpa was still alive, but that when you die, you leave your body, which is like the temporary hermit crab's shell. Rocky cried.

Later I felt it necessary to stand up in church and talk about the funny and good things my dad had done in his life. I had fought him for so many years that for my own healing, I needed to come to peace and remember the good. The night before, the thoughts and memories flowed. Many good memories surfaced. It was my duty to tell people of the compassion and kindness my father had shown others. The money, gifts, and jobs he had got people that no one knew about, and his great gift of humor. They needed to know it wasn't all craziness, all the time. I, the daughter, had to stand up for the last time and set the record straight. At the time, I thought it was for everyone else's ears, but I realize now it was for my own heart's healing.

At the grave site, as Jackson was getting into the limo, he jumped on my lap, pressed his face to the window to see the casket, and said, "So how does he breathe in there?"

"Well, Jackson, when a person—" I started to say.

He interrupted me, "I'm hungry."

When Rocky went back to school, he matter-of-factly told a classmate that he wasn't afraid of dying anymore because his grandfather would be there for him. Was he fearful or anxious on some level because of their common asthma bond? He did mention that he was sad and cried at times about his grandfather, but

I had trouble addressing his emotions with him. Unlike Rocky, I didn't cry over my father's death more than a few times, so all I was able to say was, "Don't cry; he's in heaven watching over you, caring for you like your angels."

I thought Rocky was just being his theatrical self again.

They were starting to learn about death, as I had when I was young. Hopefully it would be a slow trip, down a gentle road. Would any of these memories help them later through life? I knew my small losses during childhood, coupled with my spiritual beliefs stemming from a mix of meditation classes, lectures on Buddhism, prayer, spiritual workshops, and the powerful inner peace I received when attending mass, helped me develop an understanding of death. Jackson and Rocky had already dealt with their first small loss, months before, when our canary, Tweety Bird, had died.

Steve and I had been away for a few days when the kids called to tell us about the canary. They needed to have a burial service for him.

"Let Mommy talk to the sitter, honey," I said.

"Anna, can you bury the canary and have the kids say a few words?"

"No way, I cannot do that, Mrs. Vicky."

"Well, then, put the canary in a ziplock bag in the freezer downstairs, and we'll have a service when I get home on Monday," I said.

"You crazy."

"Yes, I know. Thank you, and don't let the kids see."

On Monday, the whole family went to the freezer to get Tweety Bird out of cold storage. As I journeyed down to the basement to get the bird out, of course I had an entourage, curious to see what a frozen bird actually looked like, following me.

"Look; he's not dead. He's sleeping with his legs up," Jackson said.

"He's frozen, stupid. You can't defrost him anymore," said Rocky.

Off we went to the flower garden, dug a small hole, and buried Tweety, and we all said a few words about his life with us. Rocky ended the ceremony with a Hail Mary, which made me smile. After all, it was only a bird.

◆ ◆ ◆

Fourth grade is a real development stage for kids. Their bodies are changing, along with their attitudes toward the opposite sex. In the first half of fourth grade, girls are dumb; in the second half, they aren't so bad. One weekend, Rocky got invited to a birthday party at a classmate's house. It was the first time he really studied himself in the mirror. "How is this shirt, Mom? Does it look okay?"

"You look great, Rocky. Are you nervous about the party?"

"No way," he answered, a little embarrassed.

Later when I went to pick him up, the mother told me they were all in the basement, dancing with her older son and friends. As I walked down the carpeted stairs, it seemed a little dark and quiet. I turned at the base of the steps, and there was my son slow dancing with a girl from his class, a girl other than me.

"Rock?"

"Mom?"

I couldn't have been more shocked if my son had been dancing in a topless bar as a Chippendale. Stunned and immobile for a minute, I mentally shook myself into reality and came to my senses before I embarrassed him. Mumbling to myself about what I had seen, I stumbled up the stairs to our friend's kitchen. When had everything changed?

"They're slow dancing down there."

"You're kidding," she said.

It turned out that the older kids thought it would be fun to have a slow dance contest for the fourth graders. Maybe it wasn't good to mix older kids, a dark basement, and music.

Why did my father come to mind? "Don't do as I do; do as I say." I had done similar things but had been a lot older, and the temptations were a lot more innocent back in the pioneer days. Everything was on warp speed now.

That year Rocky's class started working with less fortunate kids in a Head Start program, reading to them and playing. On the first day, I asked Rocky how it had gone—did he like his new little pal? Rocky turned to me with a sad face. "All the kids paired up with their pals but me. My little guy wouldn't talk to me or play; he just sat under a table. The teacher said maybe he was shy and to give him another chance. I was trying, Mom. I tried everything. I was the only one with a problem."

"Rocky, I'm sorry. You've had a bad day, but I'm sure the teacher was right about him being shy. You'll see."

After a few more disappointing trips, the teacher gave up and told Rocky that next week they would have a new little boy for him.

"You tried, Rocky; it wasn't your fault."

The following week I eagerly awaited the good news.

"So, how's that new little boy working out?"

"Well, Mom, let me tell you. Everyone is out playing and reading, and once again my new pal is under the table. I say, 'Come on out, little fellow. Let's play. I've brought you a present.' Guess what he says, Mom?" Tears were forming in Rocky's eyes.

"What?"

"He said, 'Fuck you, kid!'"

To Rocky's amazement, I burst out laughing. He stared at me. "Rocky, it isn't about you; it's just the way he was raised. Not everyone has a life as nice as yours. Be a little generous, and learn from this experience. Don't take this so personally. Things just happen, and we have no control over them. It is actually funny when you think about. What a story you can tell your friends about Head Start."

"Yeah, Mom. I guess that *is* kind of funny."

He needed to be reminded that everything was not about him and that he could turn moments like those around with a different perspective.

This litany of events avoids the real story, but in some small way, our lives did turn out well. With the help of family, friends, humor, and grace, we, like others with disabilities, became closer. It's the only way you can make it through. The ones who are out there with no one can easily slip though the cracks; love seems to be the glue that lets you get up every day and try again, and I know from experience that even a kind word from a stranger is at times a lifeline.

We were good parents. Jackson was a good brother. We overcame those stressful years, and we traveled and laughed a lot. We had good friends, a fine school, loving teachers, and a dog that listened. But it didn't matter.

Rocky died anyway.

Chapter Fifteen

It had been a great weekend. Rocky had gone to dinner with his dad and me and then on to meet his friends at the movies. I remember him not eating much and saying he had butterflies in his stomach. Was it because he was going with two girls? Was it starting already? Images flash over and over again of that Sunday and the family hikes. It was a sunny afternoon, rather warm. September days in the mountains were enticing to everyone. Steve loaded the car with the kids, dog, water, snacks, and wife. He would do anything to get us moving faster. He loved the mountains.

"You live in Idaho," he would say. "People spend hundreds of dollars to come up here and enjoy the outdoors. It's a great day. Come on; you can't just sit around."

I was reading the Sunday *Times* and planning to work in the garden. The boys were into a game of Nintendo, something I didn't like them to do during the week. The only family member jumping up and down had a tail.

We knew Steve was right and that we would have a great time exploring nature and hiking, but why take the fun out of irritating him? We drove out a few miles and parked the car. We hiked up an old road and looked for animal bones and rocks along the way. Even with a little shortness of breath, Rocky was into the hike. He seemed to be getting so much better.

Steve used to carry Jackson on hikes when he was tired or lazy, but now he kept up with us all. Steve still had the backpack with water and snacks to carry, but I was responsible for all of Jackson's rocks and found treasures, which he kept putting in my pockets. He wasn't very discriminating, but why should he be if I was the chump doing the carrying?

"Mom, Dad, look at this—it's real gold!" Jackson would say.

"Let me see that," Rocky would say.

"Look, Rocky; it must be worth a lot of money, huh?"

"What are you—crazy? That's not real gold. M...o...m, tell him!"

Those little brown eyes would squint at me and search for his truth.

"Well, Rocky, you never know; maybe it is real gold. There is a mine here."

"*Right.* Yeah, right," Rocky said, turning abruptly to continue the hike.

Another rock was handed to me for safekeeping.

Two minutes later, "Hey, Mom and Dad! Look; here's an old mine. Let's go in."

"Be careful of holes and snakes. Sometimes animals have houses in there," Steve said looking at me for an opinion.

"Oh, Mom, it's so neat in here. Dad, let me show you."

"That's okay; you go. I have to keep your mother company."

Neither of us liked snakes or large furry things—better to send the kids. When they reappeared, they decided to scratch "Rocky" and "Jackson" on the side of the mine with an angular stone. I wonder if those names are still there or if they have washed away. I am not ready to go and find out.

On the way home from our outing, the boys stuck their heads out of the sunroof and laughed, the wind blowing their hair back. A teacher from school saw us pass by.

After Sunday dinner, I remember looking out the dining-room window, and watching them play basketball with their dad. I was thinking that Rocky and his dad had finally found a sport they loved to do together. I let them play a little longer than usual because Steve was going out of the country on business the next day. As it turned out, it was the last time they would play together.

♦ ♦ ♦

Monday morning we said good-bye to Steve. He took the boys to school and had a deep scholastic talk on the way with Rocky, who wanted to know what pimps were. That afternoon a friend of mine took Rocky to soccer practice because I was picking up two of Jackson's friends. The plan was that we would all meet at the field later.

It was three fifteen.

I told the boys to play on the swings while I hunted for Rocky's team. I couldn't find him. As I walked around and scanned the field again, I saw him sitting on the grass. As I approached, I realized he was sick by his familiar body language: legs crossed and head hanging down, supported by his hands.

"Mom, the cookie I had for a snack must have had nuts in it. I feel like I'm going to throw up."

What was he talking about? He wasn't allergic to peanuts. Did he have an allergy to some other nut?

I took him to the park bathroom. On the way there, he threw up in a trashcan. Jackson and his little friend had to run over and look inside. Rocky was so sick that he couldn't leave the bathroom. Every time he tried to leave, he had to run back in. He came out and sat, doubled over, on a bench with me. While rubbing Rocky's back, I was trying to keep my eyes on the other three boys, who had disappeared again.

When Rocky came out of the bathroom for the third time, I said, "Let's try to make it home."

It was very hard for him to walk. He was so sick to his stomach.

He had got ill before from certain foods, but this ill? He ate peanut butter with no problem. What was the nut in the cookie? Why was this happening?

Some foods contain nuts in a way that is not obvious. If you have asthma, your risk is greater, because you can get anaphylactic. The asthma is prone to get very bad as part of this. Mild reactions might have gone unnoticed before to warn them clearly of the danger.

Effects of nut allergy, which you or patient should notice

Hives

Swelling in the throat, causing difficulty in swallowing or breathing

Asthma symptoms

Vomiting

Cramping tummy pains

Diarrhea

Faintness or unconsciousness; once the child is unconscious, life is in danger

Death due to obstruction to breathing or more rarely extreme low blood pressure causing

Anaphylactic shock

Time is of the essence.

—Asthma and Allergy AAIR

When we got home, I sent the other boys out to play. As Rocky started to get hives all over his body, I went to look for the Benadryl. I couldn't find it. The boys came back in. Rocky, in a gentle voice, asked if they would leave and said that he was very ill and needed to be alone. They instinctively knew it was serious; otherwise, Rocky would have yelled at his brother's little friends, as he usually did. Now he was having trouble breathing and asked for his atomizer. I ran and got it. He started to get that panicky look on his face, like it wasn't helping him.

"It's not working!" he yelled.

I didn't understand and said, "It's a new asthma inhaler."

"It's not working."

Then I understood. His asthma was spinning out of control.

I ran and got the bigger machine, the nebulizer, and filled it with medicine and gave him that. It helped a little, but his breathing was still strained. After waiting a few minutes for the medicine to kick in, I realized it wasn't going to. I was starting to have that old, long-forgotten rush shooting through my body, and I could not show it on the outside. *Maybe I should call the paramedics.* Their station was a few blocks away. I had never seen Rocky have such a severe reaction. I called and said my son needed to go to the hospital; his asthma was over the top.

I called the mother of one boy to pick the other boys up immediately. I told Jackson to run out to wait for the ambulance.

I remember he said, "First I need to cut a peach."

He wanted a snack. I grabbed his arm too hard and yelled at him. Later on it would bother him that he hadn't run out fast enough. I had to explain that it wouldn't have mattered.

As the ambulance drove to the hospital, I followed behind in my car so that I could drive us home after. I called our asthma doctor, who was in another town, to ask what to do. He said that when Rocky got to the hospital, he would get an EpiPen shot, and then he should be okay. Why didn't we have our own EpiPen shots? We had been going to this doctor for years.

Why didn't the ambulance put on its lights and rush? Did I stress the asthma too much and not the cookie to the drivers? Later I found out they were not paramedics, only EMTs, who could do nothing but administer oxygen. When you see an ambulance, you just assume your community has paramedics and they are capable of extending or saving a life with all their equipment.

When we got to Emergency, Rocky received the shot and two treatments for asthma. He said he felt a little better. He looked calmer to me, which made me think everything would be all right. The doctor stepped out and left us with the respiratory assistant.

Rocky was lying there with an oxygen mask on when, all of a sudden, he curled up in a ball toward me and screamed, "I can't breathe!"

I yelled to the nurse, "Give him another treatment! Give him another treatment!"

He said, "I can't without the doctor. He already has had one."

I was losing it now. I was holding my son's face while blindly searching my pocket for his atomizer and then trying to spray it in his mouth. The mist was not going in. He was unable to respond by taking a breath. The mist was like a lowland foggy cloud hanging over his lips. His eyes—those huge, sensual eyes—were beyond pleading; they were looking to me for help. Then he stopped. Silence. He couldn't take in any air. The doctor ran in, and in the longest minute of my life, he proceeded to put tubes down Rocky's nose.

Anaphylactic shock is a severe allergic reaction. Histamines and other molecules are released into the bloodstream, rendering ordinarily water-tight blood vessels leaky. Tissues throughout the body swell, tightening the airways (and sometimes collapsing the lungs) while dangerously lowering blood pressure. In addition, rashes, retching, shortness of breath, swelling of the tongue and the throat might occur. People in the early stages of a reaction often feel profoundly that something is very, very wrong, just as they feel the first hint of an itch.

Time is of the essence: death may occur within minutes

—The New York Times

That's the moment I play over and over and over—the twisting of his body, the look of panic in his eyes, my clumsy attempt to give him medicine, that mist across his mouth. The last words he spoke. "I can't breathe." It comes back every day, every waking minute.

It was about five thirty. His body had shut down. I stayed in the room while they worked. There were many doctors now. The room was crowded with people who had children, people who knew me. It was a small town. I remember this tremendous burning in my chest. Fear.

I had the nurse make two calls for me: one to a doctor and one to my best friend. I thought of my friend who had given him the cookie. I could see the pain in her face. What could I say to reassure her? It could have been any one of us, at any time, giving him something that would push his body over. Who could have known?

I could see and feel the tension and worry in the emergency room, but thought to myself, *They don't know my Rocky. He fools them every time.*

Then I heard someone say, "Call the hospice people. Does she want a priest?"

Why would I need those people? Just for comfort, I guess. I heard them tell a lady in the next room that her son would have to wait. They were in a serious emergency. The woman peeked out. She was a friend from school. She stared at me with alarm. I wanted to comfort her and tell her it would be okay.

Then I heard, "Where is her husband?"

I thought, *Why bother him? He's on his way to South America. I can handle this. It's like the other incidents over the years.*

I heard someone say, "We need to find him."

Rocky was filling up with carbon dioxide. His lungs were not working. They needed to put a tube in his right lung, which had collapsed. They couldn't give him any more meds; his heart was pushed to the edge. They were taking his clothes off; he had urinated in them. Now he was lying there naked as they put a catheter in him. There seemed like a dozen tubes coming out of all parts of his body. I was going to have some story to tell him tomorrow.

Someone called the Catholic priest. Father John arrived, nodded to me as I stood at Rocky's feet and went right over to him. Leaning close over my son's face, he anointed him, making a small sign of the cross on his smooth, small, forehead while praying ever so softly near his ear. Seeing a gray-haired priest praying over my son while doctors worked around him and listening to the inaudible, rhythmic sound of his last blessings pierced me. I was an outsider witnessing an intimate act between Rocky and God. There was no room for me as mother or caregiver. Those days were coming to an end as I stood in that emergency room at the foot of my son's gurney. When the priest finished, he looked up and said he would pray for Rocky.

Was God testing me again? He couldn't possibly want Rocky more than Steve or I. I silently spoke to God and begged him to help my son. I prayed to Rocky's angels and my angels. I prayed to the Blessed Mother, who knew what it was like to see her son suffer and die. I prayed to all my dead relatives, especially my grandma. *Don't take him. He is only ten, with a full life ahead.* Someone would listen; we were good people.

The doctors tried everything. They all had young children. After some time, our doctor asked me to follow him to a waiting room to talk. Eager to lend support, all my friends jumped up and followed me down the hall. The farther down the corridor we traveled, the more serious I knew it was going to be. In an undersized waiting room, I spied a set of plaid hospital chairs and sank down into the worn foam seat as if I were a robot. The doctor sat and turned to face me.

Inches from my face, he stared intensely into my eyes before he began to speak and made sure that what he was about to explain would sink in. "It doesn't look good. We have one more thing to try, but it's a very slim chance."

You hear this, but the information does not go past the ears. It stops above the heart. They were going to try and stabilize Rocky and airlift him to a major hospital, fifty-five minutes away. The Sun Valley hospital had done all it could. There was only room for me in the front seat of the helicopter. There was no way they could have left without me.

My friend was holding his clothes and shoes. His clothes were stained, but I thought, *maybe I should take the shoes for the way home. Clothes are always easier to buy than shoes.* Then I thought, *what the hell? We'll get new shoes, too.* Then I thought, *how will he go to get these clothes and shoes when he leaves the hospital? He will be naked and shoeless.* You think about such crazy, unimportant things at times like this. It's your mind's way of protecting you.

I heard the loud whirr of the helicopter landing outside the hospital. Everything seemed so surreal, like I had become a figure in a dream. They were still trying to stabilize Rocky and collect and transfer all the tubing and IVs.

As I was put in the helicopter, I watched my unconscious, sweet boy being wheeled out. My hands would not let me perform the simple task of closing the seat belt. The pilot learned over and buckled me in like a child. I couldn't slam the door shut. As he got out, he closed and secured it. He explained to me that only he could communicate with the medical staff monitoring my son in the back of the helicopter. If I needed an update or had questions, he would relay them to the team. If only I could have held my son's hand. I needed to touch him, see him, and connect in some small way. It was going to be a very long hour.

Then raising his hand slowly, the doctor touched the outside of the helicopter window, his hand fitting the curve of the glass. Our eyes met. It had been hours since we'd started this journey together; there was nothing left to be done or said in this hospital.

As we were about to lift off, I could see everyone standing in the background, illuminated by the emergency sign. There they were, blowing kisses our way. They were not the kisses that were tossed out when leaving a party, filled with fun and mischief, but kisses held together by sadness and fear, sent out slowly and gently, willing the helicopter forward and up with love. They stood there—some in white uniforms, others in car-pool clothes of sweaters and jeans—waving and holding their palms together in front of their lips as if in prayer. Steve had been reached and would meet me many hours later after traveling as fast as he could. I was really scared for my son now.

People would later say, "You did that alone?"

Even if you are surrounded by everyone you love, in a moment of crisis, you are alone with your child, your baby, as one. You are in a small box together, with room for no one else. Time seemed to be running out.

Chapter Sixteen

There is a saying, "You are alone with the alone, and it's his move."

I was in the hands of fate, by myself, and it was God's move now.

It was a long flight to the Boise hospital. The team with Rocky kept me up to date from the back, telling me his blood pressure was still at such and such. I couldn't bring myself to ask if that was good or bad. I sat there staring straight ahead and tried to will the hospital lights into view. A short time later the pilot pointed out the hospital's flashing light ahead. We came in for a landing. Emergency crews were waiting, bent over. No, this was not a television emergency show; this was the real thing.

I waited while both teams conferred, exchanged paper work, and transferred IVs. Rocky lay on a gurney about six feet away from me. I couldn't go closer; I was frozen, unable to step forward. This could not be my life. While the helicopter rotors continued to beat above me, I strained to hear what the medics were saying. I needed some sort of clue, but the blades drowned out their words. Suddenly they rushed him into the hospital.

I was told that I would have to wait in the waiting room. I objected strongly. I told the nurse I had seen everything with him through the years.

"I held him when he had his circumcision. I held him through stitches, IVs, millions of blood tests, allergy tests, seizures and asthma attacks. I can handle this. I won't get in the way."

She would not waver. I felt like a caged animal. First I couldn't hold or touch him in the helicopter on the way over, and now this.

I paced back and forth and kept up my begging and pleading. All of a sudden, a nurse bolted through the double doors and said, "The doctor wants you right away."

I ran down the hall. It was such a garish, bright room. Rocky was on the table. Someone was manually pushing on his heart. His skinny feet were hanging out, the ones he always bought shoes too big for, which made him seem to have clown feet. I started to kiss those feet again, and I kept talking to him. At one point, I felt him lifting away from me. Our deep bond, that umbilical cord of love, was floating farther and farther out. It was as if you were at the airport watching a loved one fly away. You didn't know when you would see them again. You stood guard at the window until that plane became a tiny dot and then disappeared on the horizon.

I said, "I know your angels want to take you, but don't leave me." I felt awkward saying this out loud, but I had to. I felt that the harder I tried, the harder they would try. They say the hearing is the last to go. The doctor looked at me then turned to the nurse and said, "Let me try."

He started pounding on Rocky's chest. It now seemed violent. Then he paused and looked at the monitor. It was a flat line. He told me he could continue, but it wasn't good.

He also informed me that Rocky was not getting enough oxygen. I asked for a few minutes to whisper in my son's ear, to tell him of my deep love, of how I knew it was his choice. He would be okay now, but I wouldn't. I told him to help his father through this and to come to Jackson in a dream, because at such a young age, he wouldn't understand the death of his brother. No one could, and while he was at it, not to forget me. I would need a lot of dreams. We would all be devastated for a very long time. I then told the doctor to shut everything down.

I saw the nurses crying.

The doctor reported, "I discussed his status with his mother, who was at the bedside throughout the resuscitation. Because of his absence of any cardiac function throughout an hour of resuscitation, further therapy was felt to be futile and support was discontinued. The patient was pronounced dead by myself after a total of sixty-one minutes of CPR. The cause of death is anaphylaxis, which progressed to respiratory arrest and cardiac arrest. The coroner has been notified."

I heard a voice from outside the door say time of death was 11:35 p.m.

I was asked to step outside a moment so that they could take out the tubes and clean him up. After a minute, I went back in and stood by him, holding his face and kissing him all over. His cheeks were cold. It was as if he had been out playing in the snow, all excited and out of breath, with stories to tell.

Where was his scent? They had wiped him hospital clean. I didn't want him sanitized. He didn't have his Rocky fragrance anymore. I buried my face in his hair. There it was, familiar and comforting. The hair that had grown to his shoulders and been tied in a ponytail, bleached, moussed, and buzzed; that musky boy's sweat, the perfume of youth.

How many times had I told him he needed to wash his hair? I now could not breathe in enough to last forever. Someone brought me a chair and I sat down as close as I could to him and laced my fingers through his. I remember stroking him and thinking how easy it was to curve his hand down over mine as if he were only resting. My crying was from some new place very deep inside. This was not real. This was not happening to us. Why, God, had we come this far, gone through this much, to have this happen to us now?

I sat there for a very long time, just Rocky and me with my hand resting gently on his head. A parade of people started coming into the room, people who had jobs to finish up so they could get home. It was past one in the morning.

First on the list was the chaplain. Even though he was kind, I couldn't connect with him. He seemed more awkward with death than I did. I asked him why they had put gauze patches on each of Rocky's eyes. I was told that it was in case we wanted to donate his corneas; it had to be decided quickly, and those patches kept his eyes cool. It was hard to think of someone operating on those beautiful, big brown eyes. Those eyes, my son's eyes, that could break a heart and get a thousand favors with just one look. I was also asked to consider donating his heart valves.

How could I make these decisions without Steve, Steve who was still in the air flying, Steve, who didn't know yet that his son had died?

Next came the coroner. Was I satisfied that Rockford died of anaphylactic shock? "Satisfied"? Someone tell this guy to pick up a thesaurus. Did I want to step out while he took some pictures? No, I did not. I kept sitting and holding Rocky's hand, but I put my head down on his chest while the coroner lifted the side of the sheet to take pictures. Tomorrow they were taking class pictures at school...

Next was a kind nurse, who asked if I wanted to lie down for a while before my husband came. It was now after two. I was led to a sleeping room for mothers down the hall. When she opened the door, I could see someone else settling in the adjoining room. What was wrong with her child? I would trade her. The two rooms were separated by a private bath and had a small twin bed in each. It reminded me of my college dorm room.

I couldn't help but think how nice this hospital would have been when I'd had to stay with Rocky when he was little, when the only choice had been to go home or sleep in a lumpy, plastic chair by my child's side.

"If you need anything, you just call us," the nurse said.

"I'm so cold," I said.

"Let me cover you with this blanket."

"I don't want to miss my husband coming in; he doesn't know yet..."

"We'll watch for him. You get some rest. Do you want me to keep the bathroom light on for you?"

"Yes, please."

The nurse covered me like a baby. I curled up in the fetal position and wished to be held and taken from this night. I wanted my son.

I needed to go to the bathroom, but I had nothing left to make the effort to get up. This was not happening; this was all a dream.

I remembered a beautiful Buddhist saying, "Dying is like waking from a long dream." Was my baby having sweet dreams now, never to have pain again?

I lay there for a few minutes, but then I started to worry that I would miss Steve coming in and some stranger would tell him the news. I pulled myself up and went down the hall, back to Rocky. Another visitor came, a different nurse who had just come on the floor. She wanted to know how long I would be in the room because they had to move my son. I asked, to where? She said the morgue. This really got me. I said that I didn't see a line forming to get in here, and secondly and most importantly, I was not meeting my husband and taking him to the morgue to see his son. Exit new nurse.

I wandered across the hall to the nurse's station to watch for my husband. They offered me a juice and a cookie to go with all my Tums. I obliged them for the sole reason that I thought it might remedy my severe stomach pains that I had acquired at the first hospital. In a trance, I sipped from my box of apple juice and studied the swinging double doors at the end of the hallway, as I kept an eye out for Steve while I looked at my son lying so very still directly across the hall.

While I was still in Sun Valley, I had made two calls, one to my mother for prayers, and the other to Sue, whom hospice called for me. I could never think of Laurel's number even on a good day, and I knew Sue would relay the emergency to her and Frank. Now hours later I had to call them with the fatal news. Standing there alone, I spied the nurse's phone sitting on the clean Formica counter and asked to use it. I wondered if the nurses were aware that I was making long-distance calls. I needed to talk and share the burden of grief with my loved ones and, maybe subconsciously, make it reality.

Someone came by and said, "I think your husband is getting off the elevator." I took a deep breath. What resources were left in me to be the bearer of this news? I glanced at the nurses to visually confirm what I had just heard and headed out of the comfort of their station. I raced down the hall through those double doors, and as soon as Steve saw my face, he knew and broke down. We held each other for a long time. He put his hand in his satchel and pulled out a box of Junior Mints that he had brought for Rocky, his favorite movie candy.

Finally, arm and arm, we slowly made our way to Rocky's room as if we were a reticent bride and groom heading to the chapel. We entered the room and Steve gazed upon his son. He could not understand. I had gone through this ordeal all night, but Steve had the extra pain of arriving after Rocky had died. He had just seen him off to school. How was this possible? It was after three in the morning. After some time, I told him about the request for Rocky's eyes and heart valves, and he said, "Of course," without hesitation. I loved him for that.

The hospital tried to find us a room for the remainder of the night. Because of a convention in town, they could only find an old, worn-out hotel. Shouldn't you be awarded a deluxe suite for this? The chaplain drove us there. We stood in the lobby as he checked us in, and I wondered if he told the clerk about our tragedy. It was our first contact with people outside the hospital.

Once in a room, we lay down on the bed, too stunned to talk with each other. At about four thirty, we fell asleep for about a half hour, and then we had this strong desire to get back home, a two and one-half hour drive. We called a cab to take us to the car-rental lot. The cabby left us in the taxi and went into the hotel to talk with the desk clerk. I am sure he was checking to make sure we weren't ditching the bill. Why else would two people leave so early with no luggage? I wanted to yell at him, "We didn't skip out on this lousy hotel. Our son is dead. How dare you add to our burden by checking on us?" But that thought was overlapped by one that said, "Who gives a damn what you think? Everything is meaningless now."

It was a long drive home. We were dreading the talk we were going to have to have with Jackson, who was staying at a neighbor's house. How do you tell a seven-year-old about his brother's death? How can you explain what has just happened when you can't explain it to yourself? We had called a few friends and family members, but our talk with Jackson would be face-to-face and with the person closest to us.

I remember walking up the cement steps to our neighbor's house. With a lump in my throat, I raised my hand to knock on the heavy wooden door when it suddenly opened. No one could face each other for more than a brief second for fear of crying—you could see it by their tightly held expressions—nor could we embrace for fear a flood of tears would begin. We knew the task at hand needed strength, and seeing friends could really make us break down. Jane, who was Hank's mother, said, "Jackson's upstairs with Hank watching television. They don't know anything yet. I kept them both home from school." As my husband and I climbed the stairs, we tried to hold it together.

Jackson and Hank were taking advantage of a day off from school and didn't care to ask any questions as to how or why they had earned that perk. Opening the door, we spied them sitting on the show-no-spills corduroy sofa oftentimes used for sleepovers. As Jackson looked up, I said I needed to talk to him.

"Hank, come downstairs with me a minute. Jackson needs to talk to his parents alone."

Jane closed the door, and I asked Jackson to sit down between Steve and me. I took him on my lap, and as his little plaid-shorted legs hinged over my own legs, I put my hand across his soft scuffed knees and my arm around his shoulders and pulled him closer.

Looking deep into his eyes I said, "Jackson, Rocky was very sick. The doctors couldn't help him, and he died in the hospital last night. He is an angel now."

I can still see that little sweet face, which had been just laughing a few minutes earlier. At first, it took a second to register. Then he put his head in my lap and sobbed. We cried together. After a moment, he asked if I was sure Rocky had died. Later he told me he thought that I was going to say, "Rocky's in the car. Let's all go home. You've missed enough school."

At home at last, I went upstairs to my bedroom to take a shower and get off the clothes that I had worn since the morning before. It was the first time that I had been alone since the initiation of our tragic journey. All of a sudden, I had this overwhelming feeling come to me from Rocky. I was in the midst of pulling off my sweater when I was compelled by his presence. It was as if I entered a sacred sanctuary and was filled with light and peace. A higher source was telling me that I was not alone.

This experience put me in a place of insight and privilege and helped me recognize my son's presence. I was swept over by a deep, warm feeling of love, like a spiritual embrace from a parent to a young child. Rocky told me that he felt so free, and the feeling he wanted to convey was more than happiness. He had returned to his pure essence. It was joyous. The emotions he gave me at that moment were as if I had just watched my son win the Olympics. I was engulfed with his grace. He was free of his body and soaring. My sweet boy was comforting me, and someday it would be bearable. I would be okay.

Chapter Seventeen

Everyone asks us what it's like to lose a child.

Disbelief

How could it be? This only happens to people you don't know who are on the news at night, in some town you have never heard of before. "What a shame; how tragic," you say to yourself as you reach for your magazine and think about making dinner.

Anger

We'd finally got it right. Why us? And this is hard to admit: why not someone else's child, one who wasn't so handsome and smart, who hadn't had such a tough childhood? Why didn't he come home from the hospital this time like all the other times? Why was it different this time? What could we have done to change this?

People cared and were concerned for us, but they went on with their lives—the school plays, the ski trips. I pictured people at cocktail parties or restaurants sitting around and kindly discussing details about Rocky's death or how we were doing as a family. They also needed to speak about our tragedy so that they, too, could make sense of the whole shocking incident. My friends certainly had their emotional moments, but they slept most nights. They planned family vacations over coffee. They looked at colleges.

What about me? What was I suppose to do? How was I supposed to act when they forgot and talked about their kids' parties or school trips? I knew they cared and were careful in their conversations around us, but my whole body and soul, my whole existence was the loss of Rocky. It was a quenchless yearning that couldn't be filled.

Steve and I took turns sitting with Jackson. He had never fallen asleep easily. Now it was even worse. Sometimes we would be so exhausted, we would fall asleep next to him waiting for his eyes to shut.

One night a short time after Rocky died, Steve was rough-housing with Jackson. Jackson, who had crept around all day watching parents, teachers, and friends cry, needed a moment of fun. I lashed out. "I'm glad you two are happy!" How cruel of me to say that. I knew it, and I tell you, I didn't care. I wanted to strike out at something or someone. I wanted to inflict pain. I succeeded. Jackson had been jumping on Steve's back, clinging to his shirt, while Steve smiled and reached around to pull him off and toss him high onto the twin bed. Steve tossed Jackson one more time and said, "We'll play later, buddy." Was I happy now, having brought them back to the reality of the moment?

Relationships
They say that 80 percent of marriages don't make it through the death of a child, and I can see why. No one grieves the same way. If you are having a fairly good day without any major breakdowns and come home to a sobbing spouse, it makes you angry. If you have worked hard to move ahead by just a bit, your spouse can bring you down with one look. If you are having a bad day and your spouse is up, you get angry, as if to say, "How can you think of being happy? Our son has died. Don't even dare to laugh or smile." It is a no-win situation.

The only connection my husband and I had was the bond of deep grief. We were unable to comfort each other; there was no holding each other in bed at night, no kisses or embraces.

Steve would go in and say good night to Jackson, whose bedroom was down the hall from us, and then after having splashed some water on my face and carelessly brushed my teeth, I would follow. I would sit on Jackson's bed and try not to pay any attention to the empty twin bed beside his. The room decorated with denim comforters and large flag pillows also included mounds of stuffed animals and Beanie Babies. The reason we had so many Beanie Babies is that every time Rocky and Jackson went to mass with me, they could buy one after church. I personally didn't think Jackson was into the "stuffies," as Rocky called them, but he always wanted to do what his brother did. Slowly he would have to start finding his own way.

Jackson automatically turned over on his stomach for one of my famous mommy back rubs, which I did to relax him and see if he wanted to talk. As I rubbed his small spine up and down, he would finally turn his head to the side. That was my signal to work on his ears, neck, and head. Sometimes he would ask questions while I was massaging; sometimes I would ask about school or friends in order to bring him out and continue to keep my finger on the pulse of his emotions.

"Did Rocky talk in the helicopter?"

"No, Jackson, he was not able to talk; it was sort of like he was sleeping."

"Oh..."

And that would be it for the night, except for "Can you sit here for a while?"

"Yeah, I'll sit here."

Other times when Steve and I got into our own bed, we would lie on our backs, knowing the other was awake but unable to break the thick silence between us. What was there to say? After a while, we would turn away from each other and try not to cry out loud. We pulled the down covers up over our shoulders, but they were of no comfort. They could keep out the slow seeping, like an IV drip, of such deep sorrow throughout the darkness. During the night when we woke, we realized that this nightmare was ours and not someone else's. We could sense when the other was awake, but like coming out of anesthesia, we were too paralyzed to move toward each other. We were like stones made of sadness and pain.

Once in Jamaica, I remember seeing a mansion by the sea. Over a hundred years before, a wealthy plantation owner had built it for his bride as a surprise. It was called a "great house". It took years of planning; the view over the Caribbean was breathtaking. Finally the house was finished, and just before he took his new bride in, he realized that the workers had used salt water with the mortar instead of fresh water. The salt water made the house crumble and erode. There it sat now; it was called the House of Folly. Is that what would become of our marriage? Would this death placed upon us become like the salt water, our catalyst of ruin? We spoke few words unless it was something we needed to deal with concerning Jackson. At a time when we needed the most love, we got and gave the least to each other.

Steve would sit on our deck over the river for hours on end. Our deck hung over the confluence of the Big Wood and East Fork rivers. We had replaced the wooden railings, and they now gave you a feeling of floating over the water. It was very calming and Zen-like. Steve sat there, reading book after book. He told me this helped him not to think of our tragedy. He couldn't speak. Sometimes I would pull over a lounge chair, wrap myself in a blanket, and stare down at the tumbling water or the Mallard ducks on the other side of the bank. I would sit next to my husband and want to talk about that night, about what it was like before he'd come. However, with one look at his pain-ridden face, I would become quiet. It was as if our physical proximity was a magnet for pain. In some ways, we acted as if we were from two different countries, sitting in an airport lounge. Not speaking the same language and knowing we wouldn't see each other again, there was no need to try to communicate.

The economy shifted again, and Steve's import business started to change. In our grief, we were unable to make decisions when needed. Now we had new business dealings to worry about as well. Everything reminded us of Rocky, and nothing else seemed important, except for Jackson. We needed to reach out and move ahead for him, no matter how slowly we went. My mom used to say, "Problems are air soluble," and I believe that to be true. Women talk; men internalize. Only one time did Steve get angry and lose his temper with me. I had bought a bag of almonds for snacks. As I was putting them away, Steve snapped at me, "How could you bring nuts into this house after all that has happened to us?"

I stood there, unable to react to his behavior. I had never thought about it. I couldn't process what he was saying. It was so out of character. As time went by, the nut issue disappeared. In retrospect, I don't ever think it was about me bringing nuts in to the house. It was his total helplessness about Rocky's death, not being there at the time of his death, and the nuts, like so many other things, just triggered it.

The more I talked and cried about Rocky and that night, the more accepting I became that nothing would bring him back; for some reason, our lives were meant to go on without him. Thank God for patient friends and family. Overall I think men like to mull over all their problems first by themselves and then go forward with partial solutions. I couldn't wait that long. I felt like I would burst with pain and stories about my beautiful son.

When we have those fresh breaking hearts, we can only hope to survive minute by minute as if we were addicts getting through the day. As time goes on, we must embrace our spiritual connection and try to accept our losses. We cannot bury our grief. We must work through it by any means, whether prayer, mediation, or just talking to someone who cares about you.

Mark Nepo wrote a beautiful book, *The Book of Awakening*, about the heart breaking, which is something that we cannot avoid. He basically says that when our hearts are broken wide open by pain, that is when God's grace flows through us. We need to empty our assumptions about our lives to start anew. Facing our pain is not an easy task, but the tears that come will fill the fissure with grace.

I needed to incorporate and face my pain in my daily life and to constantly take slow deep breaths to move on inch by inch, until I could become a survivor and not a victim.

I began to write and go to mass more often. Someone told me of a clairvoyant in the area; maybe in the future I would call her. I didn't want people to think of me as the Whoopi Goldberg character in the movie *Ghost*, but it wasn't their concern anyway. No one has the right to judge someone else's suffering or his or her way of seeking comfort, and shame on anyone who does. You have the utmost right to do what works for you. No one else will ever come close to feeling what your pierced, broken heart feels like.

People offered these words of solace: "You are so lucky to have another child."

Does a person walk around with one shoe if the other is lost? Is the table set with the pepper and not the salt? My children were a set; they did everything together. Every photo showed two boys with a smile, not one. How were we to feel about the face that was no longer among the family snapshots? On car rides, what would happen to the little boy sitting alone among those unused, dangling safety belts, talking to the back of my seat instead of bantering with his brother? And what would I do with my vacant hand flying in the air as my young son and I ran down trails or into oceans? How would it get used to that weightless, aching void that had been filled by Rocky's hand? Something was altered; order was gone, and it was as if the winter didn't have the spring to follow. How could I explain this emptiness to anyone? Just as one could not understand the feeling of riding a bike by reading a book, neither could one feel the sting of death by witnessing someone else's pain.

One evening Steve was away on an important business trip. Jackson and I sat across from each other at our long antique dining table. It had originally been a draper's table for laying out bolts of fabric and seemed to stretch endlessly on down the red dining-room wall. We were like two tiny cartoon characters sitting at one end of the pine table. Behind us stood a wall of art photos punctuated by two windows and yet-another caged canary. I'd lost track if we were on Tweety Two or Three.

Due to the time change, the blackened evening skies were making us feel even more alone and vulnerable. We felt abandoned without Rocky, who was usually the entertainment when Steve was away. I thought back to how Rocky tried to get Jackson to sit at the table when we'd bought it at an antique show. Jackson wouldn't eat at the table the first week because he said it smelled weird. It had no odor, but still he couldn't be convinced until Rocky interceded by clowning around and made him want to sit down with us.

Jackson was intrigued by the way Rocky ate dinner. He went slowly around the plate eating each item, finishing it, and then going on to the next; moving from the potato, bypassing the corn, and heading for the steak. That was his system. Jackson went for the vegetables and salad first, which Rocky thought was "totally" weird. Now it was quiet.

Jackson and I were like an old married couple, fumbling to keep the conversation going, each of us empty and running on fumes from the previous week.

"How was school today?"

"Okay."

"Did you have your favorite gym class today?"

"No, Mom. That's not till Tuesday, remember?"

"Oh, I forgot."

"It's okay, Mom."

I didn't want to be responsible for anyone. Everything was overwhelming: homework, making school lunches. I couldn't even think up a lunch, let alone make it. Cooking dinner was a burden. People offered to cook for us. I couldn't figure out what time for them to bring food; I didn't know if we even wanted food. It was too much, so I just said no. Then when it was time to feed Jackson, I wished I had accepted, if only for his sake.

Each day we tried harder to please each other, role-playing to find a groove. We were like a puzzle with a missing piece. I wondered how Jackson was really doing, deep inside. He always held a lot in; he was so different than Rocky, who was in your face about everything. I talked about Rocky to Jackson often, in a gentle way, so that he would feel free to talk with me and not be afraid that his questions about the death of his brother would be the catalyst for more grief.

The morning after Rocky died, I asked Jackson to take a shower with me.

Deep in our own thoughts, we stood under the shower. Placing my hand on my heart I said, "I feel empty inside; do you?"

He tipped his little seven-year-old head up to me and nodded.

I said, "We will work together to fill this large hole inside us."

We stood there in silence, letting the water pour over our bodies for quite a while, closed off and contained in that small shower stall. We knew that opening the door meant getting dressed and continuing on; neither of us was ready for that journey.

He didn't want to sleep alone. He was afraid that he would forget how to breathe while sleeping. I knew this related to Rocky's asthma. Ten years old used to be safe—not anymore. If a ten-year-old could die suddenly, why couldn't a seven-year-old, like him? What about his mom and dad?

He wanted to know if Rocky's birth mother knew he had died. I explained that I didn't know where she was and had no way to contact her. Did Sizzle know Rocky was not away for just a few days but had died? I believed she did and said so. She was Jackson's dog now.

This was different than Grandpa's death. Grandpa had been far removed from our everyday lives and hadn't lived with us. It was important that I allow Jackson to ask questions about his brother, about what happens after death, and that he felt able to express his fears and thoughts to me. I needed to be calm and honest. Some people want to protect their children from the reality of death. It is extremely hard to express your thoughts about death to anyone, let alone your own child, especially when it was his brother who had died. This death was so close to the bone.

At times, answering a question about the night Rocky died and what happened was terribly difficult for me. Tears would roll down my face, and my voice would crack. Jackson needed to know that it was okay to cry and be sad, and that it was okay to tell funny stories and even laugh during this period. That even adults can't be above such matters. It was called grieving. He needed to work out some questions and feelings his own way. My job was to be his support system.

We sent Jackson back to school after only one day out. We thought it would be better for him to be with his buddies than to watch a bunch of adults cry in his home. The school had had the hospice people meet with every class the day before. When it came time to share something in class that day my quiet Jackson said, "My brother died." How brave of him.

The Funeral

We waited a long time for Rocky's body to be brought back to our town from the Boise hospital. That same day the phone rang, and I picked it up. It was a telephone salesman about to make his pitch.

"So how are you today, madam?"

"Not so good. My son died yesterday."

There was a slight pause before he hung up.

What was I thinking, making remarks at a time like this? After the mortician prepared Rocky, they called us to come and see him. That, I think, was the most difficult trip. I was hoping he would look the same, without any bruises or signs of trauma from his organ donations.

Huddled together on the cracked mortuary sidewalk stood my mother and friends in a vigil. Steve and I walked up the few cement steps arm in arm. My chest felt as if it were about to explode with fear, pain, and unspeakable grief. As we entered the vestibule, a dark-suited man greeted us and escorted us down the sedate hallway into a small room, which held a simple wooden casket. Everything was in a dream state of slow motion. The funeral director opened the casket ever so gently. It was as if he were opening a priceless box containing a rare jewel. There laid our sweet child, looking so handsome and pure. I thought my heart would burst from my chest and go flying around the room in that instant.

We alternated between staring at him and clinging to each other, sobbing. You cannot take enough of him in. You stroke him. You kiss him. You step back and gaze at him. You move in and stroke him again. You put your hand over his hand. You straighten his favorite warm-up suit around his neck. It's not that it needed straightening, but that's what you, the mother, always did. Then after standing in silence for a time, you ask your few dear friends and mother to come in so you can present your beautiful child to them. So they, too, can witness this impossible moment. So they, too, can see what you have lost.

You want them to suffer with you.

They do.

We went home to pick up Jackson. I told him that I had just seen Rocky, that we were all going to church for a few prayers, and that if there was anything he wanted to put in the casket, he should get it now. I would help him decide. He thought very hard about this. To him it was a big responsibility, and he had to get it perfect. They were in the midst of the Pokemon game craze, so Jackson picked two cards that were Rocky's favorites, a framed picture of Sizzle, Rocky's dog, and a box of Junior Mints, Rocky's favorite movie candy. He rode to the church next to me with all these items on his lap. How would he react when he got there?

As we entered the church in Sun Valley, there stood the lone, modest casket at the front of the altar. It seemed to be dwarfed in the dim lighting, dark walls of wood, and lofty ceilings. Our friends and family stood back to let the three of us have a moment alone with Rocky. Jackson went up to the casket and stared at Rocky. Had it helped that he had been to my father's funeral? He asked if he could touch his brother. He said Rocky's face was cold. He tugged on Rocky's hair. He tried to move the corner of his mouth. I wanted to stop him, but I held back, afraid to intercede. My friend Sue gently reached over to take his hand.

He placed the cards and candy inside, and then he moved them to the other side of the casket. He studied his results, and then he placed the picture up against the back, moving it twice so that it sat up properly. This job was very important to him, and you could see him wanting to make his part of the contribution perfect. He went to sit down during prayers. During prayers, he got up by himself and went to stare at Rocky. Our friends all watched Jackson as they continued to pray and wondered what he might do. How could he understand? None of my talks with him could ease the shock. I could see him trying so hard to digest his brother's death. As we were leaving, he decided that Rocky didn't need the framed picture of Sizzle; it was his dog now. Driving home, we were all so drained that everyone was quiet, thinking his or her own thoughts, happy not to make small talk.

The next day was the funeral. Where would we get the strength and energy? Back at home our dear friends busied themselves bringing out an endless supply of food. How could I say that, even though I had little appetite, I was comforted by the mounds of provisions surrounding me, the food, the soothing, universal bond, beginning with a baby's first calming suck of milk? Even the missionaries knew to feed the natives before they attempted conversion. Christenings, wedding, bar mitzvahs, even the Last Supper. We have always gathered together to celebrate and support one another in this way.

I found it amusing that each food item matched the personality of its giver. The Southern friends brought cola and soft drinks. The Jewish friends brought deli and soup. The Irish brought stew; the Midwesterners brought fruit pies, and a friend who owned a great bakery kept us in bread. All were so gently human, trying to help ease our pain in some small way.

My two dearest friends Sue and Laurel, magically appeared from California as I was sitting on the sofa staring out the window. Everyday they kept themselves busy cleaning the kitchen, preparing food, and making drinks. I sat there watching as they sometimes whispered to themselves and glanced my way. They

had been there in the beginning when I changed Rocky's first diaper and Sue had said he had a tiny penis. They had met us during
hospital emergencies, had attended his baptism and birthdays,
and had laughed and kidded Steve when not even the adults
could break the piñata he had purchased. We went on vacations
together with all our kids. They had Rocky's first baby snapshots
proudly displayed on their refrigerators and walls. What had gone
so wrong?

The friends staying with us from out of town kept themselves
busy finishing up details of the funeral. They collected, without
our knowing, small river rocks, which they hand-painted with a
silver *R* as keepsakes for people to take home. The flower arrangements kept pouring in. Someone brought in the stack of
mail. There on top was a postcard from my favorite photo gal-
lery in New Orleans. I starred at the black and white photo in
disbelief. It was an angel with a flowing hazy gown. In the angel's
outstretched hands was a rock. The photo was titled *Angel of
Light*. We all stood staring down at the picture. Later my friends
purchased the original photo for us.

This tragedy had a life of its own. It was moving ahead with
or without us. Friends went through all my albums to select pictures of Rocky for a video. Occasionally I would pause at one
and remember. We found a poem he had written in first grade.
People busied themselves with jobs and made more work than
necessary; they labored over every little detail. When they began
to banter back and forth about which style of *R* to put on the
rocks, I told them they needed another funeral to work on. They
had too much time on their hands. Once again, expressing one of
my nervous jokes to make them feel at ease.

They had all put their lives on hold for us. Just having them
there was such a comfort. They would listen with those familiar
faces and hold me with those familiar arms. Everyone was well

aware that tomorrow was the day and that we needed all our strength for each other.

What was there to say? The day was here. We slowly showered; neither Steve nor I could talk. The only time we became animated was when Jackson entered our room. Steve reached for his dark business suit and white shirt. I couldn't decide. I didn't want the usual depressing funeral outfit, but most of my wardrobe was, by choice, dull and dark. I stood in the closet for the longest time and stared at the hangers, but my mind had drifted some place. Finally I pulled out a navy pantsuit.

Jackson came in and wanted to know what he was going to wear. We went into his room, where he selected shorts and a T-shirt that Rocky had liked. I would have thought that I would have insisted on more formal attire, but it didn't seem important then.

Steve and I moved in slow motion, as if coming out of anesthesia. When we got to the church, so many people were standing around the entrance. On each side of the entry door there were tables for signing in and baskets of "Rocky" rocks as a remembrance for people to take with them. Not wanting to talk with anyone, we moved through the crowds and went directly to the back of the sanctuary where the coffin was, away from everyone. There were so many people honoring our son, but it was all a blur. While everyone was taking a seat, we stood guard over Rocky. I felt a new fear lancing my heart. This was the real separation time; after today, I would not see or touch him again. I asked the funeral director if he would open the coffin one more time. He did. To look again, the yearning, when would it seem real? Rocky was touched, kissed, and memorized. It was time. I would not see him again.

The casket was closed for the last time, and we—my husband, son, and mother—followed behind the pallbearers. There were so many friends. The church was overflowing. I could feel the embrace of all their eyes watching us. There they sat in the oak pews in utter shock as we moved by. There were blessings and songs, and then Rocky's classmates got up to talk. How courageous they were, ten-year-olds standing in front of the crowd. They seemed way too young for reminiscing about their funny, loving friend with their small and sometimes-shy voices. They gave us such a keepsake that morning. A parent talked about Rocky and her son's friendship, how they loved the movies and how if it wasn't at least a PG-13, Rocky wasn't interested!

Letters that I had received started drifting through my mind as I sat and stared ahead.

From a parent:

> I loved and admired Rocky. He possessed wonderful qualities and was mature beyond his years. His ponytail in the second grade and his obvious comfort with his willingness to be different demonstrated his independence and his sense of himself. I feel privileged to have known him pretty well...He always "held court" at our dinner table on a variety of subjects with great relish and humor and insight and never ceased to be interested in any subject or open to any thought. (A great, great quality!) He was terrifically funny...I am sorry and sad for my son who adored Rocky...I looked forward to their growing up together and teaching each other...Rocky was special and had an openness and emotional complexity and honesty that most of us should want to emulate. He accomplished a lot in his short life and I, among many, am better for having known him.

From a girl in class:

I am thinking about all of the fun times we had with Rocky. Once we were playing horses and Rocky was the guard dog and kept all the enemies away. Another time was in second grade and we used to put pigtails in Rocky's hair. I never forgot at my birthday party, Rocky danced with all of the girls in a circle and all of the girls were fighting over who got to slow dance with him. Rocky always had a smile on his face and always had love in his heart.

From his teacher:

As his teacher, I want you to know how much Rocky touched all of the children's lives. There is not a single day that goes by in which Rocky stories are not told. The expression that is often heard in class is, "That is so Rocky!"

From a mother:

I knew what Rocky liked for after school snacks and always had those mini hot dogs on hand. I pictured our boys growing up together, dating the same girls…I will always miss Rocky's smile, his songs, and his dance moves…sharing his tenth birthday with my son, teasing me about being too emotional, crying during movies. Boy, I bet he's laughing at me now. I can't seem to stop crying.

Handwritten notes meant so much. I clung to them and reread the memories people wrote down about my child—funny incidents, kind acts, things I didn't even know about, another side to my child I was never aware of until now. At times, I would fill a bath and sit surrounded by Rocky stories. I remember one night softly crying while reading a note from a woman I hardly knew. She was touched by Rocky's kindness. The mother wrote in a condolence card that Rocky had introduced himself to her and her two children at the golf club pool.

"I will never forget the day when my boys and I had the privilege to meet Rocky," she wrote. "We were sitting by the hot tub, and Rocky asked, 'Are you new here?' He welcomed us and told us what a nice community it was here in Sun Valley.

"Though faces were starting to look familiar, it was so fitting that Rocky extended himself. I was so impressed with his contagious personality, infectious smile, and warm spirit. Ever since that day, we looked forward to seeing Rocky, especially at church when I had to hush the boys, as they would say, 'There's Rocky.'"

Another card read, "These words were spoken by Puck to Rocky's character in the play...'The Queen as her attendant had a lovely boy, stolen from an Indian King; she never had as sweet a changeling...She crowns him with flowers and makes him her joy.'

Rocky had been in *A Midsummer Night's Dream* with the senior kids, whom he loved. Even though he'd had no words, he had showed up every day for hours of practice as the Indian boy.

As I finished reading, I placed the letter along the side of the tub, and leaning back, I slid down just so my head was above the water. Then I started to think how easy it would be to gradually slip down to the bottom, but that wasn't in me. After a while, I slowly moved up and reached for a towel. I had another child I loved dearly and a wonderful, broken husband both who needed me to be strong and fight through this nightmare. I went downstairs and started dinner.

After everyone spoke at the funeral, they showed a video of Rocky's life in photos, accompanied by his favorite song by the group NSYNC, "God Must Have Spent a Little More Time on You." All these moments combined to make a true celebration of our son's life.

When we got to the cemetery a mile away, the pallbearers— who included Frank, Sue's husband, Murray, and my brother— brought the casket out. They carried it up a beautiful green hill and set it under a large leafy tree. I liked the idea that birds would be sitting by Rocky and keeping him company. It was the older part of the cemetery. There were worn gravestones the size of shirt boxes sticking up, most tilted back from age and weather.

Suddenly the funeral director whispered in the pallbearer's ear that a water pipe had broken and that the grave area was filling up with water.

Steve tried to kid and said, "Rocky never had it easy."

No one knew what to do.

"Do we want to leave him in the hearse and bury him later?" said the funeral director.

Were they kidding? Leave him in the car by himself and go off to lunch?

Finally we were told that the cemetery crew had discovered the problem and fixed it. I always wondered if they were just saying that to move us along. After the burial, surrounded by friends at the car, I gazed back and saw all the children sitting around the grave, throwing in flowers and chatting to Rocky. There they sat with each other, carving a spiritual notch in their souls.

The reception that followed was a blur. What I remember is being mesmerized by beautiful stitches on the suit a man was wearing while he was talking to me. I remember some people coming up to me to express their sadness and some people staying clear in the distance. I looked around at all the white tablecloths with beautiful flower arrangements and trays of fruit and sandwiches. People were in groups, chatting quietly, drinking coffee, and looking over toward me once in a while. I had no idea where Steve or Jackson had gone. Finally I was driven home and slept all afternoon, except for a moment when my little Jackson came to the top floor of our house to look at me up close and touch my hand. He was dealing with his own fears. Tomorrow would be better. We knew it could not be worse.

Emptiness

In the beginning, you need so much holding but not those bone-crushing, wrestling holds. Some people would come up to me, start sobbing, and squeeze me tight, burying my face in their chest so I had trouble breathing. I needed to be treated like a baby with small rhythmic pats on my back, but I didn't even know that at the time. No one is well versed for those unimaginable moments. Many people were working through their own fears. It was human.

When the people who had experienced the loss of a child came up to me, locked eyes, and then hugged me, it was different. We had an invisible, electrical connection. They bore witness to me that, yes, you do live through this staggering disaster. You will continue to live and breathe and move through this unpredictable thing called life. As if they were angels in disguise, there they were in front of me, looking like everyone else in the dresses and suits with no telltale marks that said, "I, too, have lost someone." They stood there wearing the look of survival. Would I do the same?

Later I met a mother who had lost a child.

She said, "Can you believe how thoughtless people can be in what they say to you?"

I don't believe that anything said is thoughtless. People are only trying their best in an uncomfortable situation. Everyone who approaches you is nervous and wears his or her humanness on his or her sleeve. Some are just better at verbalizing it.

Going to the grocery store was hard. I would later make a joke of my encounters. Boom! Going down the fruit and vegetable aisle, a familiar couple would turn the corner and catch sight of me. It was the deer-in-headlights look. I could see what they were thinking all over their faces: "Damn, I told you we didn't need bananas. Now look what we're up against: the Bateses. What are we going to say? What should we do?"

I saw their eyes darting back and forth as they tried to see if there was an escape route behind the fruit display. If I were in a generous mood, I would avert my eyes, get deeply involved with the contents of my purse, and give them a chance to escape.

Again at the grocery store, a neighbor was buying cookies for his daughter's class party. When he saw me he said, "Boy, I almost got cookies with nuts, but I put them back, remembering Rocky."

I'm sure it was his way of connecting with me, but it sounded like he wanted a prize for his quick recall. I nodded with a smile, took my cart around the corner, and stood against the pancake-syrup shelves; I was intent on getting on with my "normal" shopping excursion. Instead, I felt that familiar feeling of physically wanting to vomit my pain. I longed to slowly slide down that pancake-syrup wall to my knees and be swallowed up by the clean linoleum floors.

I wanted to lean against those bottles and be rocked, like a baby, back and forth, by all those Aunt Jemimas until the pain quieted in me and I could face the checkout clerks and lines of familiar faces again.

Ten years before in another grocery store, I had wanted someone to compliment me on my beautiful newborn son. It didn't happen. This time was different. I didn't need reassurance; I needed my son. It is always better to say something than not. Even a touch on the hand is enough. When people don't acknowledge your loss, you wonder if they know, if they care.

Chapter Eighteen

I woke up. It was morning. My son was dead. It's a strange first thought, like, *Oh, it's morning; I better get up. What time is it? My Rocky's dead.* He was not at a sleepover, not at camp, but *dead*, never coming in my room again. He will never wake me up by doing the hula with that green towel around his waist. He was so good at the hula. He picked up the dance on a trip we had all taken to Hawaii the year before. He had decided to learn after watching with amazement the dancing girls wearing coconuts for tops at a hotel show. With his Elvis Presley hips, he could out move any luau showgirl.

The next day when Jackson came home from school, he went to Rocky's room and took all the Pokemon cards and Rocky's cashbox of money.

When he saw my curious expression, he said, "It's okay, isn't it? He doesn't need them anymore." He went upstairs with his new treasures, put them on his desk, and drew a picture of the whole family, including the dog and the canary, playing basketball. Then he tacked the picture on the wall, right by his pillow.

This gave me an idea. The next day I went out and bought a loose-leaf folder, drawing paper, and stickers of different events. One night when Jackson seemed especially quiet, I pulled out all my purchases and said, "Let's make a memory book about Rocky." It was a way to work side by side. Talking about Rocky was comforting. Rocky hated fruit but bragged that he did indeed eat fruit, even though we knew it was once a month and was only a bite of apple or piece of watermelon the size of a quarter!

"Let's draw a page with all of Rocky's favorite fruits."

Jackson looked at me curiously. Laughing together, we proceeded to draw watermelon bubble gum, a cherry lollipop, blueberry cotton candy, and grape gummies.

During our sharing, I brought up all the mischievous things Rocky had done to Jackson, and we laughed some more. I was aware of how easy it was to make a saint out of someone—all those kind words uttered, the son who now could do no wrong. Jackson didn't need to feel he had to fill a space in our lives. He carried his own light within.

I pulled out camping stickers, and we did a page with drawings about one of our camping trips, which brought up more good memories and stories.

Then Jackson said, "I wish I had one more day with Rocky. I didn't get to say good-bye. It seems like a dream. Did he say anything about me before he died?"

Oh, how I wanted to make something up. Nothing came to me, except that flashback of those few frantic moments that kept playing over in my head.

Later Jackson would have that dream I had asked Rocky for. Jackson was home, sick with a cold, and worried that he'd miss his hockey game the next day. He sat down by me on the sofa to cuddle. "I don't want to die," he said. "It's forever." We talked about God, angels, and reincarnation.

"I liked Rocky," Jackson said. "We had more good times than fights...He was funny."

We watched an old video of Rocky and Jackson when they were little. Rocky was pushing Jackson around and around in a baby walker; they were both laughing for the camera.

That night Jackson had his dream. He was in an ice hockey game, and Rocky was his goalie. Rocky magically lay across the net; laughing, he flipped back and forth and saved all the goals.

He even helped Jackson get a goal in. It was a joyful, playful dream. When the game was over, Rocky told Jackson that he had to go. Jackson said, "Rocky, what's it like in heaven?"

Rocky said, "Jackson, it's the best place. You listen to your favorite CDs and dance and laugh all the time. I love it!" Then Rocky laughed and went straight up into the clouds.

The next morning Jackson came running in to tell me about his great experience with his brother and his favorite sport. He looked happy.

Rocky had answered my request the night he died.

A child can only take in so much at one time. The same holds true for adults. Jackson would bring up one question about dying, and when he'd had enough on the subject, he would jump up and say he had to go and feed the dog or call a friend, any excuse to get out of the conversation. Which was normal.

Every day was an emotional dance. You could move up two spaces and then back one; up one and then be at a standstill for days in sadness, followed by good days. It was always different, never predictable. It was the dance of mourning.

It was essential that Steve go back to South America for the business trip he hadn't made the night Rocky died. He didn't want to leave us; it was too soon and too much like reliving that night.

Jackson and I said, "The heck with school for a week. Bring on those mileage points." We all needed to go, and we did. It was the same route my husband always took. Salt Lake City to Atlanta, Atlanta to Santiago.

"Flight two-three-eight to Santiago is ready for boarding."

The gate agent approached my husband. "You don't remember me, but I helped you get a flight back to Idaho the night your son was in the emergency room."

As she smiled down at Jackson, she addressed my husband with warmth and said, "I'm so glad your son made it through."

With tears welling up in his eyes, Steve said, "He didn't make it; he died. This is our other son."

The agent started to cry along with us. There was no safe harbor for grief. So many miles away, from Idahowhereisthat? in Atlanta, late at night, pain still could find us and a stranger who happened to work for Delta.

♦ ♦ ♦

Time passed.

An early snow dusted our lawn. As I went out to get the morning paper, I looked up at the sky and realized it would soon be Rocky's eleventh birthday, followed by the Christmas holidays. Those days were hard, but not as hard as the days that take you by surprise. It's like being shot from behind without warning.

Driving in the car, I would suddenly hear Rocky's song on the radio and envision him dancing in the seat next to me, as he used to on the way to and from school. Or I would pull up to school to pick up Jackson, and there I would see some of Rocky's classmates kidding around and playing. Oh, what searing pain. I was no longer a part of that club; fate had kicked me out.

At home, it was odd going down the hallway past his room. I felt a craving, an invisible pull, as I went by. At his desk, I was surrounded by photos of his friends, his walls covered in movie posters.

Idly, I opened his desk drawer and pulled out his secret life. It was the life that was Rocky Bates, the individual, not defined by "son" or "brother," but a person emerging on his own. There were candy wrappers, Mexican money, plastic monkeys from some exotic Roy Rogers drink, and a Jamaican knit cap with attached dreadlocks. I picked up the hat and deeply inhaled his aroma.

There was a tiny piece of paper with two stick people that said, "Cheer up, Rocky!" Did a girl write this? Pencils rested quietly side by side with the name "Rocky" on them. I remember when Santa got those. I ran my finger across his name. I pulled out five brightly colored rabbit's-foot chains, which he had won at a video arcade; I now know they do not work.

I slowly slid open his closet door. There was Rocky's new leather jacket hanging alone on a cheap plastic hanger.

A few weeks previous, we had been to Boise for a little back-to-school shopping. As we walked into the kid's Gap store, Rocky spied a leather jacket and pulled it off the rack. I thought to myself, *are you kidding me? a kid's leather jacket? No way.* I turned away to help Jackson find some pants and thought that Rocky would move on to something else.

As I looked over the brightly colored sweater pile, I spied him slipping on the jacket. As he pivoted left and right in the mirror, he caught a glimpse of me behind the sweaters. He gave me those big doe eyes and wordlessly said, "Mommy, have I told you what a good mom you are?"

About twenty minutes later, after his father and I talked about the value of money, Rocky expounded on the fact that, number one, it was on sale; number two, he could wear it a few years; and, number three, he would generously hand it over to his little brother (who had absolutely no interest in clothes).

The first time he wore it was a Saturday night. Two girls from his class had invited him to a movie. He really looked handsome, and as he turned to say good-bye, he looked at me, smiled, and kissed me on the lips. He had never done that before, and it sent such a strange powerful energy through me that I just stood there as he bounded down the stairs to the awaiting car. To this day, I remember that feeling of that kiss. I hadn't known at the time that nothing would be the same after the weekend.

Sometimes, the physical reaction to death is very intense. Out of the blue, you start crying, with not even a thought of your child to set you off. You feel like you could vomit from deep inside; it's a great heaving of all your pain, as if someone had taken his or her two hands and literally pulled your chest apart. You are always tired and many times cannot focus. You could easily see how some people would lose the desire to continue.

I understood by my own loss that extreme sorrow is almost an out-of-body experience that I could drift into the unknown to be with my love so easily, without regard for anyone else.

I dreamed of Rocky twice. Each time, I would be embracing him and telling him I wouldn't let him go until he promised to come back. I woke up every night and went over and over the moments with my son. I looked out the window one night and saw a shooting star. I said, "Rocky, if that's you, give me a sign and do it again." I saw seven shooting stars in a row and went to sleep. Once, I woke up, and he was calling me. I got out of bed to look for him. Everyone was sleeping. When I meditated, I could feel my son sink into my being and calm me with his spirit.

Once, I decided to get out of the house and get some fresh air. Sizzle and I headed down to the river at the end of our street where she could swim and I could think. After a while, I said, "Rocky, give me a sign you are here." Upon returning home, I found a sparrow sitting by my front door. I picked it up. It turned its head toward me, sang a single note, and then flew away.

My friends reacted to my feelings and experiences with anything from crying to that look that was a mental pat on the back, where you know they are saying to themselves, "Well, if it makes her feel better, humor her."

We decided to go away to Mexico for a week. People said, "Aren't you afraid to fly together?" I found this amusing. Since we had lost a son to a cookie, a plane ride certainly wouldn't concern me. When we got to the hotel, we immediately wished we were home. There were no children for Jackson to play with. His traveling companion was missing. He would have been better off at school with his friends. When a hotel clerk asked Jackson why he was out of school, Jackson wanted his dad to say that his big brother had died, something my husband would take a long time to verbalize to anyone.

Steve was working his torment out by himself. I wanted to tell the story over and over until it would be as if I were repeating a recipe. I would sit by the pool and hope someone would say, "You have only one child?" That would be my opening.

When I went for breakfast one morning, I said to the waiter, "*Buenos dias, como esta?*"

He said, "Oh, senora, I have to work very long today."

At that moment, I wanted to grab him by the lapels and say, "You think you have fucking problems, buddy?" Where did this anger come from so quickly?

In a store, when I went to pay for something, my wallet opened to a picture of the boys. The saleswoman said what beautiful children I had. Pointing to Rocky, I blurted out, "This boy just died." She didn't know what to say or do. I had made her so uncomfortable with my own uneasiness. I later learned just to say thank you and keep quiet. What do you do when people ask how many children you have? I found out it depends on the person you are talking with and the extent to which you wanted to connect with them. It all hinged on how much I felt like sharing that day with another person. I knew that if I mentioned my son's death, it would lead to a lengthy narrative.

As time went on, my need to talk lessened.

During that trip, the three of us took a taxi into Cabo San Lucas. Steve kept asking me, "Are you sure that door is locked? Check it again." Jackson was sitting by the car window to take in the view. Steve had to make sure he wouldn't lose another son.

"It's locked, Dad; don't worry," said Jackson.

Would this be our new way of life? I could not live life operating out of fear every day, waiting for something bad to happen to us again. I wanted our old life back.

Chapter Nineteen

As I was standing at my son's grave a month later, a gray sedan full of older people pulled up. Two women with beehive hairdos and a man with red suspenders clambered out with their cameras. They wanted to know where Hemingway's grave was. I told them it was around the bend. My husband saw trouble and headed back to the car as I stood by Rocky's graveside. One woman approached me and asked, "Do you have someone buried here?"

"My son."

"How old was he? What did he die of?" Her friend was working her way over the hill.

I said, "He was ten, and he died from anaphylactic shock."

She said, "I never heard of this; I can't even pronounce it."

I told her, "He died of an allergic reaction."

"I am so sorry, dear."

Knowing Steve would ask why I had bothered to engage in conversation with people peering at graves, I left them clustered under a tree and made my way to the car. As shocking on some level as that was to me, on another level, they reminded me of my aunt who made a career of visiting and talking to relatives and friends, dead or alive, at the cemetery. They were just simple old folks out for a ride and an early bird meal. I couldn't fault them. Certain exchanges just weren't important anymore.

We attempted to return to the things we might normally do. We went to the bar mitzvah of Sue and Murray's son. We attended only because they were dear friends. It was too soon for us.

During the ceremony, the parents were chatting about their fine son becoming a man. Tears filled Steve's eyes.

Confused, Jackson turned his face toward Steve and asked me, "Why is Daddy sad?"

I said, "Jackson, they are talking about Zach becoming a man, and Daddy is sad knowing Rocky won't have that chance."

Jackson looked at me, thought for a moment, and said, "But Rocky wasn't even Jewish."

Out of the blue, Jackson went into post-traumatic stress syndrome. As feelings ebbed and flowed in our house, he seemed to be doing better at school. One day on the way to school as we passed the hospital, Jackson had an attack.

"Mom, I can't breathe. What's wrong with me? Feel my heart; it's pounding so hard, and I'm scared. I need to get out of the car. I need air."

We were in bumper-to-bumper morning traffic. I scanned the side of the road and tried to spot a place to park. Easing over to a grassy section in front of an old house, I stopped the car. Jackson opened the door and jumped out. Keeping my eye on him, I reached for the door handle and then ran around the front of the car to comfort him.

"I feel like I'm going to die, Mom. Feel my heart; I'm not breathing."

"Jackson, stay calm; you will be okay. Your body is breathing for you even when you think it's not. It's always working for you day and night, even when you're sleeping."

As the cars zoomed by on their way to school and work, all I could think was, *what's next?* I was angry that God was neglecting us by piling more trouble on the shoulders of this innocent boy. Here my son and I stood, south of Ketchum, while people slowed to see if they could help. I saw a neighbor with a can-I-help-you look on his face, but I waved him on with the back of my hand.

This wasn't fear Jackson was feeling; this was anxiety. With fear, your emotions are directed toward something in particular, like entering a new class, starting a different sport or job. You know what it is that worries you. With anxiety, you have an overpowering feeling of helplessness. You can't figure out what's wrong, but you know you are losing control of the situation. It is a severe feeling of panic. Jackson thought that he was going to die soon or that his parents were going to die and leave him. Anxiety put him in this state of mind.

Could there possibly be any more surprises in store for us? Was it passing by the hospital that triggered his fears? It was a new hospital, one that Rocky had never visited. Looking up panic disorder on the Internet, I read that an attack appears suddenly without warning and that attacks are terrifying. It is the person's response to the trauma he or she has experienced. The hospital was a reminder of Jackson's losses, and trying to avoid thoughts and feelings brought on by that reminder only worsened his condition.

Not being able to express his depression and true sadness over the fact that his big brother was no longer going to be at school with him also added to his fears. All week Jackson had me stay at school with him. He would get claustrophobic in his classes and run out, panicked and crying. He needed to sit by the window or exit door. The teacher was kind and patient and explained Jackson's feelings to the class when Jackson wasn't around. I felt mixed emotions—helpless, sad, and trapped by his needs. Why was this starting now? Why couldn't I help him?

I was gradually trying to go back to my design business so that I wouldn't have to dwell so much on Rocky. During that time, I would take business calls in the teacher's lounge. When I needed to go Jackson's classroom to reassure him, I would take him outside and hold him, but anxiety attacks don't play fair. They have no sense of honor in hugs or gentle words. Anxiety was in charge, and it quit when it was ready to quit, no matter what your age or circumstance. I was the only one who could begin to comfort him.

Jackson intuitively knew I was up for the job of tucking him in at night. I could hear Steve locking the front door, shutting the lights off, and coming up the stairs to our bedrooms. I was sitting next to Jackson on his bed, as Steve peeked his head in and said, "How're you guys doing? Do you need anything?"

I would answer, "No, we're fine; just talking."

"OK, goodnight then. See you in the morning."

"Goodnight, Dad."

"Night, buddy; night, Vic."

"I'll be there in a minute."

In our bedroom, Steve would be alone, lying across the bed and reading with the television on for distraction, while I sat in our son's room. Trying to think of some neutral ground for small talk to ease him into sleep, I would turn to Jackson. Alternating between wanting to be alone and wanting to reassure Jackson, I answered his questions about death and anxiety and realized how many things made him feel alone and isolated; the list got longer every day.

He wouldn't sleep at his friend's house, and he didn't like it when friends asked if he missed his brother. He lost interest in playing with others, and he wanted me to sit outside on the lawn chair and watch him play. He wanted to sleep with me every night. Now I was going to bed early, starting in Jackson's bed and then working my way over to Rocky's bed with its multitude of stuffed animals. Curling around a big teddybear, I would try to comfort Jackson and constantly say, "Go to sleep now; it's late." I couldn't sneak out because he never fell asleep until late. Many nights I would give up and let sleep take over me. Steve would try to step in, but it seemed that lately I was targeted for sleep duty.

My husband, in many ways, was having a tougher time getting through our tragedy than I was. Steve never wanted to leave the house or see people, especially people who were parents of Rocky's classmates.

Late fall was Jackson's turn to be special person at school. This was a chance for children to stand up in front of others and be praised by their peers. Jackson's classmates had to present a speech about the special person's talents and strengths in school, sports, and friendships. I asked Steve to go with me. He knew it was important to Jackson but also was aware that the lower school assembly included classmates and parents from the Rocky's fifth grade class.

As we sat on folding chairs against the back wall with the rest of the parents, the headmaster looked up and said, "Before we begin, let us have a minute of silence for Rocky Bates."

Steve and I started to cry, as did many others. The pain was so overwhelming and the minute was so long that Steve got up and rushed out the side door of the multipurpose room. Unable to look up or move, I sat frozen in my chair. At the end, when the children got up to leave the assembly, I hurried out the closest door and met Steve, who was waiting for me in the car. That was the last time he attended a lower-school function that year.

Since the only route to school was past the hospital, I thought a tour inside the hospital would be a good idea. Jackson liked that plan. He was relaxed during our self-guided tour but later said that he still had those feelings even when he tried to shut them out. He was afraid he would die and miss his family, friends, and dog. We discussed breathing and meditation.

Then something happened.

One day after school, I had to pick up Jackson and three other boys from the soccer field. When I got out of the car, someone yelled that one of the boys had cut his eye open on an old metal bench. It was Jackson's friend. After some deliberating, we thought it was best to take him to the emergency room.

As I was running across the field, Jackson pulled on my sleeve and whispered, "Mom, what about my anxiety?"

Walking swiftly in my focused mode, I said, "Forget about your anxiety. We need to get Latner to Emergency. We don't know how badly his eye is cut."

Jackson said, "Oh, okay."

As I drove the three boys to the hospital, I thought maybe this would be a blessing for us, since Jackson will see that people can go to the emergency room, get treated, and leave. When we got to the hospital, I took the nurse aside and explained my situation with Jackson. I asked if the boys could go into the examining room with their friend.

She said, "I think it will be okay, but I'll ask the doctor."

Jackson and Hank were working the Coke machine and laughing like they were at a sporting event.

Then pausing as if remembering why they had come, they said to Latner, who was nervously sitting with an ice bag on his eye, "Don't worry; maybe the doctors will give you a patch or glasses!" These two were a big help.

Suddenly the entrance door swung open; it was Latner's father. "Vicky, I rushed down here as soon as I heard. All I could think of were the memories this would bring up coming back to the emergency room so soon. How is Lat?"

"We're all fine. Lat will be seeing the doctor soon. Everyone is doing fine."

The nurse came in, and we all traipsed into the exam room. Every time the doctor asked Latner a question to see if he had a concussion, the other two bananas answered.

"What month is it?"

"April!" Jackson and Hank answered in unison.

The doctor wheeled around and gave the two the once over, and then he turned back to their injured buddy. "Who is the president?"

"Bush!" the two boys answered.

After I gave them a tap on their heads, they were quiet and let the patient answer.

The doctor injected a shot under Latner's eye so that it could be stitched up. I tried to get the boys to go to the waiting room, but they told me they didn't want to miss the good part.

I was physically and emotionally worn out from the day. When we got home, Jackson went on and on about never wanting stitches or a shot.

"All right, already!" I said.

He smiled and said, "Well, at least I'm over that death thing." Both of us started to laugh.

We began going to hospice for children, and through that group, Jackson saw that he was not alone, that other children get fearful and anxious, and that these fears come up when you least expect them. Other children were afraid to sleep alone. Other children worried about losing someone else close to them. Although he never spoke of it, I think he came to understand that it was good for him to be with children around his age who had also experienced a death.

Six months after Rocky's death, I went out to get the mail with Sizzle trailing along. As I was standing at the mailbox and flipping through the usual advertisements and bills, I spied a card that looked like an invitation from the children's hospital where Rocky had died. I opened it with shaky hands, not knowing what I was going to view. The card represented an ironic kindness; it said that they, too, remembered what had happened six months ago and hoped that we were doing all right, and then it went on to thank us for Rocky's donations.

You become confused. How do you decipher what you should be feeling with the information? Sizzle was jumping up and down, begging to carry the mail as she did every day. I pushed her aside and started to read the card. There I stood among the spring snowdrops weaving their way up through the lacy dead leaves; life continuing on. Each word penetrated my body like a steady slow drip and filled me one word at a time with such deep sadness once again:

> Please allow us to extend our deepest sympathy to you and your family over the death of your son, Rocky. You may take comfort in knowing the priceless gift your son gave helped two individuals regain their sight. Both corneas were transplanted on September 17, 1999, one in Northridge, California, the other in Indianapolis, Indiana. We are thankful for families like you who, in the depths of their grief, offer eye donation. This gift provides the only opportunity to give individuals another chance to view their surroundings and loved ones. The decision to consent for donation takes a tremendous courage and we appreciate that more than words can express.
>
> Lions Eye Bank

Another letter I received was from the hospital where we had spent our final night together in Boise. As I opened it along with the sympathy cards, I realized it was a bill for approximately $4,000, an insurance oversight. This seemed so ironic to me. Why should they send us a bill when we didn't come home with our child? If the dry cleaner loses your dress, do they bill you for the cleaning?

Suddenly everything in our lives seemed backward.

We are all connected, part of a swirling circle called life. Human beings on a path, being moved along whether we want to be or not. Some are like those dogs on the way to the vet, being pulled along with all four legs frozen to the floor. Others face what seem like insurmountable hurdles and move with grace and spirit. For most, tragedy is all-consuming. Grief has no edges. It fills you and everything around you. Everything you see, hear, or taste is a reminder of your loss. As time passes, you realize everyone has had or will have life struggles. You become aware of those who have ridden the wave. They become the beacons, the torchbearers, for others who are entering the waters of grief.

If someone had said, "Take this baby. He will have a lot of problems. Raise him to the fullest of his potential, through spirit, mind, and body, and then say good-bye in ten years," what would I have answered then? Probably no. If the question were put to me now, I'd say yes. Rocky expanded my heart with such completeness.

Many people, who looked so "regular" on the outside, shared their loss to help me. One couple lost their son while hiking. He was struck by lightning. How much we all carry. The daily burdens: abusive spouses, terminal illness, the loss of homes and jobs, the loss of a child. Someone once said that if we all gathered and unloaded a life's worth of sorrows, disappointments, and burdens and put them in a pile and then could pick up anyone else's problems or pains, we would always choose our own again.

Heroes come in everyday packages. I needed to remember that. When I was floating out there alone, without a lifeline, familiar hands reached out and pulled me into that rotating circle; they reminded me that I am very much connected. A note sent, relating a Rocky story about his kindness to others. Running into someone at a local coffee spot who told me of a personal loss they had endured that no one knew about.

Soon it would be my turn and responsibility to carry the torch for others. To shed light on that tragedy and help him or her find the way out of the darkness.

◆ ◆ ◆

A few months after Rocky's death, I was driving through town and turned on the news. I was listening to a discussion about paramedics in the area and about whether we needed them or not. I pulled the car to the side of the road as a commissioner was discussing his thoughts. He didn't think our area warranted a paramedic team because of the size of our town and the cost of training. I felt a searing arrow shoot through my heart. Didn't see a need? What about Rocky and that slow drive with no help? I pulled over and parked my car as the tears came.

Later that day I went home and wrote a letter to the paper:

> I would like to respond to Mr. Smith's comment concerning the paramedic situation in this valley. He says, "I personally, have not been sold that we have a problem here." Well, all I can say is, aren't you lucky? My family has been personally "sold." There is a problem here. My ten-year-old, Rocky Bates,

died this past fall. When I called the paramedics, I was under the impression that he would be receiving medical care on the way to the hospital.

Yes, my mistake.

He had a severe allergy attack. When the treatments I was giving him at home didn't work, I called nine-one-one. When they came, they assessed the problem as best as they could, gave him oxygen, put him in the ambulance, and drove to the hospital with no apparent urgency. No siren. No speeding. Not a life-threatening situation.

I thought everything was under control since he was in an ambulance. I assumed he was getting everything in the way of treatments to keep him alive. I learned later that when someone goes into this severe attack (anaphylactic shock), there is only a small window of opportunity to save the person—thirty to sixty minutes. None of us knew the scope of Rocky's problem, but trained paramedics would have given him a possible life-saving EpiPen shot on the way to the hospital.

If only one life is saved, isn't it worth it? Make Rocky's many hours in Emergency open your eyes to helping others. They all did the best they could to save our son. All I ask is, why tie the hands of those people who want to do so much more en route to the ER?

Like the medical director of emergency services said, "If it's your time, I want to make damn sure it is." Was it Rocky's time?

Sincerely,
Vicky Bates

The Sun Valley newspaper ran an article the same week, which asked its readers why it is that one of the richest counties in Idaho would have people fighting for their lives without the help of trained paramedics. Living in an area where people are spread out all over, it is important to have trained paramedics who can open airways, administer drugs, and give EpiPen shots on the spot. The time between the scene of an emergency and the hospital is the most critical time.

Two weeks later my friend Jill, a lawyer, called to inform me of a council meeting at which council members would vote on whether or not to pay for a paramedic team in the area.

"Vicky, you need to go down there and speak," she said.

"I don't think I can do it. It's too hard. I won't be able to start talking without crying," I said.

"I can go with you but only for twenty minutes or so. I have a meeting. You could really make a difference. You are a mother who knows what it's like to lose a child."

Shaking as I trod up the city hall steps, I went into the meeting room and took a seat near the back. Did anyone know why I was there or that I was going to talk? How could I tell my story to all these strangers? Would it even matter? My husband had said it wouldn't bring Rocky back, and he was so right. He didn't want to see me go through any more pain.

Feasibility studies were read, a fireman got up to talk, and questions were asked about the cost of having people trained. It sounded positive. My friend got up to leave for her appointment. Squeezing my hand, she whispered, "You can do it."

The city councilman scanned the room and asked if anyone had anything to add to the discussion.

I raised my hand, and the audience members adjusted their view from their seats. I stood and started to speak with a quaking voice, stopping often to compose myself. I told my story not for my son—it was too late—but for someone else's son or daughter or husband or wife who would walk that thin line of life and would need those extra minutes of care on the way to the hospital. My words seemed to give some small meaning to Rocky's short life, his sacrifice, our sacrifice.

The council took a vote and passed an amendment to have paramedics trained in our area. Our community raised money. Lives have been saved.

One person came up to me and said, "One voice can make a difference."

Other people in the room walked over to thank me, too. I had a small feeling of good, of right and necessity accomplished. Ten years previously I had stood up for Rocky in a similar room the day we officially adopted him.

Now I had stood up for him again, in his name, to help others. He would have done the same for me.

After Rocky was born, it took almost a year for us to go to court and finalize his adoption. The birth mother had disappeared without signing the final papers. While you are waiting, you wonder, will this woman who let him go so easily have a change of heart and make her claim? Maybe I was to only have him for a short time and give him a better chance at life with my love and the medical care we had available. Sitting in that courtroom and holding my son in my arms when they called out the birth mother's name for the last time was a fearful experience, especially after having Rocky for a year. Sudden loss was so close, with just the uttering of a few words: "I'm the baby's mother, and I have changed my mind." Little did I know that I would be standing nervously again in a similar courtroom, ten years later, talking about my son—this time not to give him our family name but to make his name stand for change in our community.

On the day of Rocky's adoption, the judge asked us several questions. One was "Will you raise this child with love as your own and treat him with all the benefits of a natural child of your own?"

"We will."

Shortly after Rocky's death, I was walking through a meditation garden prepared for a visit from the Dali Lama. Two monks were standing on either side of the entry. It was Rocky's anniversary, and when I looked up at them, I uttered this to the strangers: "Today is the anniversary of my son's death."

"How old was he?"

"He was ten years old."

Then one monk looked me in the eyes and said, "He had a full life."

That was such a powerful statement that it grew on me more and more as I thought about it. "He had a full life."

Rocky did get and give so much in life.

I tell myself that my tragedy in this life's journey isn't about me in the purest of sense; it's about Rocky, the person who blessed us with his presence. It's about his choice to go. It was never about our desire for him to stay. He came to us. We were a gift to each other, and only he could know when he had finished his work. Ten years was a full life for him. It's a daily struggle to honor his choice.

I lie on my bed and take slow, deep breaths. With each breath I become calmer. I quiet myself and think about a beautiful emerging light coming down into me and filling my heart with a radiant grace. I recognize my connection to a higher power. I remind myself of a beautiful saying, "The body doesn't choose the soul; the soul chooses the body."

At times, I feel Rocky with me and try to put meaning of his journey into my life. I think back to the adoption day and realize that he had been taken back—but not as I had thought. He was taken back in the worst conceivable way, a way I could have never dreamed possible. He was no one's child now.

As years passed, I came to believe that after Rocky died, he stepped outside of his identity as my child, the frail boy, the inquisitive talker, and friend. I believe he made a transition to a higher spiritual self, to his pure essence and spirit. There is so much more happening than meets the eye, so much more than we see when we are in the thresholds of grief.

It was not just about surviving the death of a child; there was something more and a paramount message of what he was all about on his journey as a human being. How does one life affect us? Believe me, it took a good deal of time and prayer to slowly step away from my trauma and begin my journey of understanding and healing.

With my experiences after Rocky's death, I realize that in the beginning, I was so tightly wrapped in the cocoon of mourning the physical child that I closed down to the most important connection: the essence of my child, his spirit. The spirit, the true measurement of person, will never die.

One sunny morning I stopped at our local bookstore to hopefully purchase a meditation CD. The owner approached me to see how I was getting along.

"Vic, how are you doing?"

"Pretty good, Cheryl."

"There is a wonderful woman visiting us from Florida; she's come to do readings. She is psychic, but her main gifts are bringing up people who have passed over. She's pretty booked up, but maybe I can get you in. She is quite respected."

If certain outsiders were listening to our conversation, they would think they were witnessing crazy talk, but I guess those were their issues, not mine.

"Thanks, Cheryl, but I feel Rocky around me all the time. Things have happened to me that demonstrate his presence. Many nights I feel a soft thud on my back, or my bed feels as if it is being gently pushed. It sounds bizarre, but it isn't frightening. I know it's Rocky. Once, I heard him call my name during the night. I got up and went to check on Jackson, but he was sound asleep."

"That makes me happy, Vicky." She paused, looked at me, and softly said, "We know he was a special boy. Well, if you change your mind, honey, let me know."

I didn't think anymore about it and headed home. Jackson would be coming back from school looking for his usual snacks in the vegetable bin of cucumbers, mushrooms, and tiny tomatoes.

A few days later I got a phone call from the bookstore. Cheryl wanted me to know an opening had come up and that people were raving about this woman.

"Vic, I feel you should see her. I think it would be good for you, but of course it's up to you."

And that is when my life took a giant leap forward. Rocky offered me a priceless gift.

Sally Baldwin had a warm, kind face surrounded by soft, wavy, shoulder-length hair and looked not like a gypsy from Romania but like a car-pool mom.

She asked what I wanted to talk about. I said I had recently lost a son. My reading began.

Looking down, she closed her eyes. As she looked up, she said, "Rocky is here now."

She began to speak for him.

"Mom, I want you know that that was the best death I ever had. The way you held my feet and kissed them at the end was so unbelievable for me. The way you spiritually let me go. We were meant to be together as mother and son. I want to tell you, Mom, that we made an agreement in spirit that we would be together and experience what we did."

"I want a lawyer; I didn't sign anything," I interrupted with my usual nervous jokes. The amazing thing was that no one knew what I had said or done in the hospital that night, not even Steve. But nothing needed to be proven to me.

Sally continued, "Mom, do you know how many people are with me who want to connect with their loved ones? Tell them, Mom, we are right here. Where do you think we go? We are all energy, and energy never disappears. They need to open to us."

Sally and I became dear friends over the years. When she started opening up her retreats to women from around the world, I became involved. I wondered at the time what I could offer, but it turned out that my experience of loss and my humor gave mothers hope that they, too, could move forward with the grace of their children.

Sometime later another blessing came about. My dear friend who had unknowingly given Rocky the cookie before the soccer practice was in tremendous pain. She had loved Rocky who had had many playdates at her house with her daughter. I often said to her, "I lost a son; I don't need to lose my dear friend, too. It was unintentional."

A few months later I ran into her and she said, "I have to tell you something, Vicky. I have been so devastated by Rocky's death and being the one who gave him the cookie."

"You are my friend," I said. "It could of happened to anyone of us. No one knew he was allergic to walnuts, including me."

"Well, I need to tell you something. The other night I was sleep-ing, and Rocky came to me in a dream; it was so real. He said that he loved me and that he and I had an agreement before we came here that I would help him leave. That was how it was suppose to be, and he was grateful. He filled me with such grace and love."

There is so much more happening than meets the eye in this life. Dying is just an opportunity to find our way back to our true selves, who we really are inside, our souls. Becoming human is a mission—a journey and an earthly schooling to discover, learn, and work our way though life's lessons, good and bad. We know that when we die, it's not over; just the human part has moved over. We the survivors miss the kisses, conversations, and hugs, but we forget that we are also beautiful spirits and souls capable of so much more unending love and grace. I think people under-stand this as they are dying and feel the calm draw to a higher source.

Rocky will always be with me and by my side for guidance. I believe that he sees me with a whole different perspective, one that is filled with love and understanding of my human fragilities. He is no longer caught up with his earthly self but has become a brilliant, guiding light to help all he knew to grow.

We don't know whether we will live for an hour or into our nineties; that is our journey. My loss has brought me many insights, and with those insights comes a responsibility to share the process with others who are struggling.

I am not afraid of death or being around people who are dying. I started working for hospice and am privileged and blessed to comfort people as their lives come to an end. Your death should be as glorious and cherished as the day you came into the world, no matter what your age. It seems as if it is a tragedy for those of us left behind, because of the physical loss, but to the ones who pass away, it must feel more like an awakening, free of pain and problems, as they return to their pure spirits.

The deep and abiding love I feel surrounded by night and day is from my son, Rocky. I truly believe that we all play a part in helping each other with our lives on Earth and our dying process. Rocky is here now to help me on a daily basis, and as I told him, "You owe me big time, buddy; the things you put your mother through!"

The passing years have brought me many insights. I've come to understand that it's not just about your life here but also about the beauty of leaving. I don't believe that death is the end. It is a launching pad back to where we started, the pure wonder and brilliance of our souls.

Open up to whoever have left you or are leaving you; feel the energy of their presence and their love. Give them permission to connect with you. You will be surprised at your emotional connection through reflection or even dreams.

I think our loved ones can help us more, since they are not burdened by their earthly bodies. They are pure souls now, without pain, judgment, or resentment. They know about the Botox injections you lied about and the chicken recipe you stole, but, guess what, they don't care. It's ok. It's all about love.

◆ ◆ ◆

As I lie down in the sun, close my eyes, and begin to meditate, a beauty comes slowly into focus, a quiet settling, deep inside. A thought, a feeling, comes to mind and then drifts slowly down to the bottom of my being. Like an object thrown into the water, I watch it move slowly down, back and forth, over the months and years. Then it lays to rest, nestled gently among my life's experiences. I feel the breeze now in a different way. It touches me like never before. It makes me stop midsentence to look around, as if someone is trying to get my attention. When spring comes, I listen for the birds as if for the first time. I look up for the origin; I am so touched, I could cry. The geese that fly so swiftly in formation seem to be on a direct mission—souls rushing to their new lives, focused, incapable of distraction, trumpeting to alert the others of their arrival.

I am calm with my thoughts. I know what is out there. I cannot be scared or taken aback anymore. I have been to the front lines, forever marked, and have survived.

Epilogue

Just because you lose a child, it does not mean that you get a free pass for the rest of your life. Life is an ongoing process. I started to move through my life, picking up one foot after another, pausing at times when I would hear a favorite Rocky story or be reminded of his constant phrase, "I didn't know that." He said that so often because of his endless curiosity.

My life was getting back to normal as the distance between Rocky's death and our daily lives grew. I still brought levity to situations, and by unleashing my humor on family, friends, and strangers, I brought back the true essence of who I was again, thanks to Rocky's love.

One thing that was strange is that there were people from our past who called to catch up, not knowing that we had lost a child. As they would ramble on about their lives and pause to say, "So what have you guys been up to?" I hated to break into their cheery moods with "Ah...Rocky died." There was no other way to say it. I felt responsible for their stunned silence. We were doing well, and I did not want to go through the whole saga again, did not want to answer questions and assure them until they could digest the information.

I was journeying forward, getting out of my own way, and didn't want to backtrack every time someone from the past called; it was so exhausting. Finally it seemed that everyone was caught up on our horrendous news, and we could take another breath.

A few years after Rocky's death, the only son of our best friends and Rocky's godparents, Frank and Laurel, died suddenly in a car accident. Within an hour, we got on a plane and flew to Los Angeles to be by their sides, as they had been for us.

I didn't think that I would be a torchbearer so quickly for someone else, but there it was, a grievous death of a boy close to us. When we got to their house, I saw that terrible dead look in their eyes. How could two couples both suddenly lose their sons?

As the years went by, I realized that all my life's experiences had given me a unique perspective and that, if I wanted to, I could come to the aide of others on their own poignant journeys. When Jackson went off to college, I started to write seriously. I wanted people to know that the feeling of being an empty, hollow vessel would be filled again with joy and sense of purpose if they slowly pursued it.

The following year I had a mammogram and was called back. I had been called back before, but this time I was handed a chocolate candy after I got dressed. Aw, what was with the candy? I had never got one of those before. That should have been a big hint.

For some reason, seeing the ultrasound didn't freak me out. It freaked everyone else out. They even had trouble using the "cancer" word with me. After finding a good doctor in Boise, I had the needle biopsy and met with my surgeon. I said, "Do you think it's cancer?"

She answered, "Yes."

There was no "Well...we'll see when the tests come back. Have a nice weekend."

Wow, I didn't think they gave out that news so bluntly. It's funny; thinking back, I didn't ask if I would die. I only asked nervously if I would lose my hair.

I was scheduled for two surgeries, one for the small mass and a second operation to check my lymph nodes. After more tests and mammograms, I went in for surgery. As they prepared to put me under, I was peaceful and felt Rocky's presence next to me. I guess I can't give Rocky all the credit, though, since I had a combination of good drugs flowing through my veins at that moment.

After the surgery, the doctor came out and told Steve that she had cut clear margins around the mass, and that was good news. I was taped up and sent home with pain pills. Steve drove the two and one-half hours home while I leaned against the car door, slept, and drooled on the faux leather, all while I clutched my ice pack to my breast.

About ten days later, I had a second surgery to check my lymph nodes for cancer. They were clean. After a period of healing, I had six weeks of radiation treatments of a few minutes every day.

In the waiting room, I saw people who really had troubles; some, who had already had chemo treatments, coming back for their third time. After six weeks, I was tired, but I graduated with honors. I later read in a cancer magazine that a study in Denmark discovered that people that lost who had children were 18 percent more likely to get cancer. They think it is the stress of loss.

When I started up again with my hospice visits, most patients I saw had cancer. I think that I had more compassion and that I related to them and their hard-fought journeys with a different perception. My ordeal had been so small in comparison. It took a tremendous amount of fortitude from each patient and strength from the tired families to get up every day and fight the battle with hope and dignity. I found that my experiences grounded me and brought lightness to my hospice patients. Sometimes in the darkness, our fears and grief are helped by humor. It becomes the flame that lights someone's candle.

One morning the phone rang.

"Vicky, this is Chris from hospice. We need you to help us out this morning and give a man a shower down in Hailey."

"A shower? I've never done that before. Will he be naked?"

"Yes, I think that's how most people take showers."

"What if he slips and gets me pregnant?"

"Very funny; he's eight-six years old."

It was weird helping this stranger undress and getting him in the shower. As he sat slightly bent over on the stool, I realized how hard it must have been for him. Why should I be embarrassed? He had been a college professor, and now someone was helping him wash and shave.

After trying to lean over the tub, I decided to slip off my shoes, roll up my workout pants, and get in with him. The spray hose had a life of its own and was going all over the place. As I washed his hair, I ran the shower hose up and down his body as if we were in a car wash. I soaped up a washcloth and gently washed his arms, legs, and back. Then I handed him the washcloth. It wasn't so bad.

Every time I gave a simple shower, a feeling of overwhelming grace flowed through me. One person touching and caring for another person acknowledged that we are all in this together.

After that I became the go-to gal for giving showers. Who would have thought it?

The hospice patients gave me so much more than I could give them. No one is immune to problems and tragedies. We have to celebrate life in all its ups and downs; it is a part of what makes us who we are in life. We have to remember the joys. For some reason, that laugh or smile lifts us up out of ourselves and propels us to start thinking about our situation in a different light, while anger and silence close us down and make our sadness exclusive to us alone. Working on a light heart, we will glow from within.

This is what's true for me. Every experience in life occurs as it should. There are no mistakes or accidents. Rocky was here as long as he was supposed to be so that we could experience each other's love. Everything is in preparation for the next steps of your journey. You always change in some way. You can be bitter and plummet to the dark depths, or you can rise above and walk down that bumpy road to embrace the grace waiting for you. You will trip and fall many, many times, but there will always be someone there to give you a hand. And sometimes it will be the grace of your sweet child. Your tragedy becomes a part of who you are, and you have to let your edges soften. The littlest things in life became meaningful, and every day is a celebration. Why does it take a tragedy to see this?

Knowing that you can't cling to anything, that there is no permanence in life, gives you a certain sense of freedom to slowly reach farther; after all, you know you have experienced the worst. You also know you can fall and are capable of getting up again. Accepting our burdens as best as we can helps us to release that tight stranglehold of what we had thought was to be a structured well-planned life. There is no such thing, and calmly surrendering is a tremendous spiritual leap for you and everyone you come in contact with.

Talking To Children About Death

(Taken from www.hospicenet.org)

If you are concerned about discussing death with your children, you're not alone. Many of us hesitate to talk about death, particularly with youngsters. But death is an inescapable fact of life. We must deal with it and so must our children; if we are to help them, we must let them know it's okay to talk about it.

By talking to our children about death, we may discover what they know and do not know—if they have misconceptions, fears, or worries. We can then help them by providing needed information, comfort, and understanding. Talk does not solve all problems, but without talk, we are even more limited in our ability to help.

Children Are Aware

Long before we realize it, children become aware of death. They see dead birds, insects, and animals lying by the road. They may see death at least once a day on television. They hear about it in fairy tales and act it out in their play. Death is a part of life, and children, at some level, are aware of it.

If we permit children to talk to us about death, we can give them needed information, prepare them for a crisis, and help them when they are upset. We can encourage their communication by showing interest in and respect for what they have to say. We can also make it easier for them to talk to us if we are open, honest, and comfortable with our own feelings—often easier said than done.

Communication Barriers

Many of us are inclined not to talk about things that upset us. We try to put a lid on our feelings and hope that saying nothing will be for the best. But not talking about something doesn't mean we aren't communicating. Children are great observers. They read messages on our faces and in the way we walk or hold our hands. We express ourselves by what we do, by what we say, and by what we do not say.

When we avoid talking about something that is obviously upsetting, children often hesitate to bring up the subject or ask questions about it. To a child, avoidance can be a message—"If Mummy and Daddy can't talk about it, it really must be bad, so I better not talk about it either." In effect, instead of protecting our children by avoiding talk, we sometimes cause them more worry and also keep them from telling us how they feel.

On the other hand, it also isn't wise to confront children with information that they may not yet understand or want to know. As with any sensitive subject, we must seek a delicate balance that encourages children to communicate—a balance that lies somewhere between avoidance and confrontation, a balance that isn't easy to achieve. It involves trying to be sensitive to their desire to communicate when they're ready by not putting up barriers that may inhibit their attempts to ask questions. We need to be honest with our explanations when they are upset. Listening to and accepting their feelings by not putting off their questions or thinking they are too young is also important. Simple answers should be given so they understand at their level and are not overwhelmed.

Perhaps most difficult of all, it involves examining our own feelings and beliefs so that we can talk to them as naturally as possible when the opportunities arise.

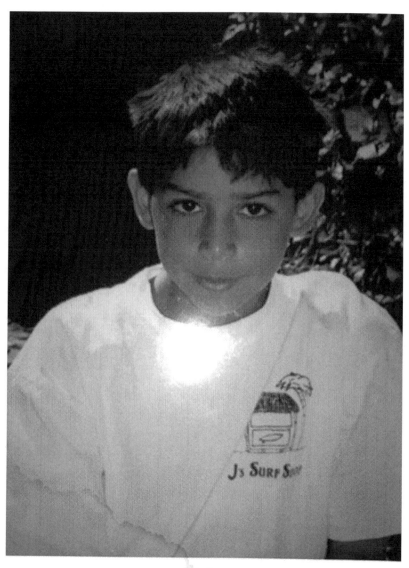

Rocky

About the Author

Vicky Bates, who suffered the loss of a child, uses her own journey toward healing to inspire others. Vicky is the founder of the blog *Losing a Child, Finding Hope* and has published articles for *Open to Hope*, a resource for people who have lost children. She also writes spiritual columns for *Woman* magazine.

Vicky strives to compassionately guide people to greater understanding, to trust themselves and their process of recovery, and to cherish the time they had with their beloved children.

47977212R00138

Made in the USA
San Bernardino, CA
12 April 2017